STEP-BY-STEP
GUIDE TO
CORRECT ENGLISH

Mary Ann Spencer Pulaski, Ph.D.

MACMILLAN • USA

TO CHARLIE

Without whose help this book
would never have been written

Second Edition

Macmillan General Reference
A Simon & Schuster Macmillan Company
1633 Broadway
New York, NY 10019-6785

An Arco Book

MACMILLAN is a registered trademark of Macmillan, Inc.
ARCO is a registered trademark of Prentice-Hall, Inc.

Library of Congress Cataloging-in-Publication Data

Pulaski, Mary Ann Spencer.
    Step-by-step guide to correct English.
    Revision of: 1974 ed.
    ISBN 0-671-86955-8
    1. English language—Composition and exercises—
Programmed instruction. 2. English language—
Grammar—1950-   —Programmed instruction. 1. Title.
PE1409.5.P84   1981
420'.7'7   81-4657
                .AACR2

Manufactured in the United States of America

20   19   18   17   16   15   14   13

Contents

Introduction 5

Diagnostic Test 7

Answer Key for Diagnostic Test 13

Chapter 1: SUBJECTS AND PREDICATES 17
Separating Subjects and Predicates 17
Nouns as Subjects 18
Finding Subjects 18
Making up Subjects 19
Verbs as Predicates 20
Making up the Predicate 20
Review of Diagraming 21
Simple and Complete Predicates 21
Simple and Complete Subjects 22
Compound Subjects and Predicates 23
Review Test of Subjects and Predicates 24

Chapter 2: MORE ABOUT NOUNS 25
Proper Nouns and Common Nouns 26
Irregular Plurals 27
Collective Nouns 29
Review of Singular and Plural Nouns 30
Review Test of Nouns 30

Chapter 3: PRONOUNS 33
Review Test of Pronouns 34

Chapter 4: MORE ABOUT VERBS 35
Present and Past Tenses 35
Irregular Verbs 37
Verbs of Being 38
Pronouns with Verbs of Being 39
Verbs Preceding Their Subjects 40
Predicate Nouns 41
Review Test of Verbs 43

Chapter 5: FOUR KINDS OF SENTENCES 45
Statements and Questions 45
Commands and Exclamations 46
Identifying Sentences 47
Review Test of Sentences 48

Chapter 6: COMPLETE AND INCOMPLETE SENTENCES 49
Complete Sentences 50
Incomplete Sentences 50
Run-on Sentences 51
Review Test of Sentences 52

Chapter 7: PUNCTUATION 54
Quotations 54
Questions and Exclamations in Quotations 56
Review Test of Punctuation 57

Chapter 8: CAPITAL LETTERS 58
Rules for Capitals 58
More Rules for Capitals 59
Initials and Abbreviations 60
Practice in Capitals and Abbreviations 61

Review of Capitals   61
Review Test of Capitals   62

Chapter 9: ADJECTIVES   63
Descriptive Adjectives   64
Predicate Adjectives   65
Comparing Adjectives   65
Irregular Adjectives   66
Review Test of Adjectives   67

Chapter 10: ADVERBS   69
Adverbs Formed from Adjectives   69
Irregular Adverbs   70
Verb Modifiers   71
Comparing Adverbs   72
Troublemakers: Good and Well   73
Adjective Modifiers   73
Review of Adverbs and Adjectives   74
More Troublemakers   75
Review Test of Adjectives and Adverbs   77

Chapter 11: MORE PUNCTUATION   78
Rules for Commas   78
Review of Commas   81
Review Test of Punctuation   82

Chapter 12: PREPOSITIONS   83
Indirect Objects   83
Common Prepositions   84
Prepositional Phrases   85
Review of Phrases   86
Analyzing Sentences   87

Chapter 13: STILL MORE PUNCTUATION   88
Apostrophes   88
Apostrophes in Possessives   88
Apostrophes in Contractions   89
Still More Troublemakers: Its and It's   91
Colons and Semicolons   92
Review Test of Capitals and Punctuation   93

Chapter 14: CONJUNCTIONS AND INTERJECTIONS   95
Conjunctions   95
Interjections   96
Review of Prepositions, Conjunctions, and Interjections   97
Review: Parts of Speech   98
A Reminding Rhyme   99

Chapter 15: LETTER WRITING   100
Friendly Letter   100
Business Letter   101
Job Application   102

Chapter 16: FINAL REVIEW   103
Conclusions   106

Answer Key for Exercises   109

Introduction

This book is designed for people who want to learn how to write correctly in English. To do this, you must learn the basic parts of a sentence. You must also learn how to put these parts together to make a good sentence. Words are the building blocks of language. This book will help you understand how to arrange your words clearly and correctly. Then you will be able to communicate with others, and they will understand and remember what you say.

Many different people—the Greeks, the Romans, the Anglo-Saxons, and the French—have influenced the development of the English language. For this reason, English may seem difficult at times. However, it will become easier as you learn how to use words to construct good, clear sentences.

This book is carefully constructed to help you discover where you need to begin your study. First it provides a diagnostic test that covers most of the material presented in the book. Answer as many questions as you can; then turn to the answer key at the end of the test and correct your work. This will help you evaluate your particular strengths and weaknesses.

The diagnostic test is divided into several sections. Each section has a heading such as *Nouns* or *Adverbs*. Wherever you make mistakes you should study the exercises covering that material. Look in the Table of Contents to find the chapters you need to study. If you make no errors in a section, skip those exercises and go on to the material that gives you trouble. You may need to study only the more advanced exercises, or perhaps only certain areas such as punctuation. Taking this test will save you time and help you study more efficiently.

You will find that this book begins with the very simplest two-word sentences and gradually builds up to much longer compound sentences. All the kinds of words we use—nouns, verbs, adjectives, adverbs, etc.—are explained and used in exercises of increasing difficulty. At the back of the book is an answer key so that you can correct your errors after each exercise and perform better on the next one. There are many exercises in punctuation and capitalization, as well as model letters for writing to a friend or to a business. Reviews are frequent, and a long final test helps you make sure that you really understand how to use simple English in its proper form. Handy tear-out pages are provided so that you can easily remove individual exercises from the book.

If you use this book correctly, you will find at the end that you are no longer making the mistakes you did on the diagnostic test at the beginning. This is because you now understand the structure of sentences and the function of the words that go into them.

The ability to use language correctly is a very powerful tool. The purpose of this book is to help you write and speak better, so that you, too, will be able to communicate effectively with the world around you.

Diagnostic Test

Take this test to find out how much you know about using English and what you need to study to improve your skills. Use the answer key that follows this test to check your answers.

I. **Subjects:** Draw a line under the subjects in each of the following sentences.

1. The boy yelled.

2. Dark threatening clouds gathered overhead.

3. Joe and Tony played catch.

4. I went to the grocery store.

5. In the dark sky shone the bright stars.

6. An eagle soared over the lake.

7. Chicago is in Illinois.

8. Julie washed the dishes and Betsy dried them.

Answer the following:

1. Why does *an* (and not *a*) come before *eagle* in sentence 6?

_____

2. Each subject in the above sentences (except in sentence 4) is the name of a person, place, or thing. What is the grammatical term for such a word?

_____

3. What is the grammatical term for the word "I" in sentence 4? _____

4. In sentence 2, find the simple subject and write it here. _____

5. Write the complete subject of sentence 2 here. _____

_____

6. Find a compound subject in one of the preceding sentences and write it here.

_____

7. Find the subjects of a compound sentence and write them here. _____

_____

II. **Predicates:** Draw a vertical line separating the subject from the predicate in each of the following sentences. Write S above the subject and P above the predicate.

1. Birds fly.

2. The team played hard.

3. The crowd shouted and cheered.

4. Maria is the oldest woman in the office.

5. Overhead roared a jet plane.

6. The day was bright and sunny.

7. In the distance we heard the band.

8. Charlie threw Jim a fast ball.

9. I am the best pitcher on the team.

10. The boys fought and kicked the intrud-er.

III. **Nouns:** Answer the following.

1. Draw a line under every noun in the sentences above. How many did you find? _____

2. Find an example of a common noun in sentence 6. _____
_____

3. Find proper nouns in sentences 4 and 8.
_____

4. Find a plural noun. _____

5. Find a singular noun in sentence 9.
_____

6. Find a collective noun in sentence 3.
_____

7. Find a predicate noun in sentence 4.
_____

8. Find the noun that is the direct object in sentence 10. _____

9. Find a noun that is the indirect object in sentence 8. _____

10. Write the plural or singular form of the following nouns.

wolf _____

story _____

radio _____

key _____

hero _____

_____ wives

_____ mice

_____ oxen

_____ teeth

_____ sheep

IV. **Verbs:** Find the verbs in the following sentences and draw two lines under them.

1. The caged lion roared fiercely.

2. It is a beautiful day.

3. High in the treetop the bird sings.

4. We were late to work.

5. All night long the baby cried.

Answer the following using the examples above:

1. Give an example of a verb expressing action in the past._____
_____

2. Give an example of a verb expressing action in the present. _____

3. Give an example of a verb expressing being in the past.

_____

4. Give an example of a verb expressing being in the present.

_____

5. Give the present or past tense of the following irregular verbs.

Present		Past	
_____	rang	_____	fight
_____	took	_____	tell
_____	won	_____	drink
_____	wrote	_____	feed
_____	shot	_____	fall

V. **Pronouns:** Underline all the pronouns in the following sentences.

1. She went to the movies with me.

2. We took them to the ball game.

3. He and I are good friends with them.

4. You can come with us to visit him.

5. They put her on the stretcher.

In the sentences above, some pronouns are used as subjects and some are used as objects. List them below according to how they are used.

SUBJECTS	OBJECTS
_____	_____
_____	_____
_____	_____

_____ _____
_____ _____
_____ _____

VI. **Adjectives:** Circle all the adjectives in the following sentences and draw an arrow to the words they describe.

1. The fat little boy ran down the dusty street.

2. That tall blond girl is the smartest in the whole senior class.

3. She certainly is intelligent!

Answer the following:

1. In the above sentences find an adjective in the predicate that describes the subject. _____

2. Give the comparative forms of the adjective "little." _____
_____

3. Give the comparative forms of "intelligent." _____
_____

VII. **Adverbs:** Circle all the adverbs in the following sentences. Draw an arrow to the words they modify.

1. Slowly and painfully he hobbled up the mountain.

2. The beautifully decorated room was very impressive to me.

3. Very quietly he walked down the steps.

Answer the following:

1. For each adverb above ending in "ly," write below the adjective from which it was formed.

_____   _____

_____   _____

  2. Is "good" an adjective or an adverb?

  3. Is "too" an adjective or an adverb?

  4. Is "there" an adjective or an adverb?

  5. Is "their" an adjective or an adverb?

VIII. **Prepositions:** Find the prepositional phrases in the preceding sentences. List below each preposition and its object.

PREPOSITIONS   OBJECTS

_____   _____

_____   _____

_____   _____

IX. **Conjunctions and Interjections:** Circle the conjunctions and underline the interjections in the following sentences.

1. Oh, darn! I hooked it, but it got away!

2. Hey, wait for Tony and me.

3. Wow, did you see that?

4. I'm late because I got lost.

X. **Kinds of Sentences:** There are four kinds of sentences. You will find an example of each kind in the preceding exercise. Write the term that tells what kind of sentence it is.

Sentence 1 _____

Sentence 2 _____

Sentence 3 _____

Sentence 4 _____

Every sentence must express a complete thought. Draw a line through any incomplete sentences below. Separate run-on sentences by using the proper punctuation.

1. First he shined his shoes then he took a shower.

2. Opening the window and shouting at him.

3. He put a sinker on the line it sank into the water.

4. As soon as breakfast was over.

XI. **Punctuation and Capitalization:** Put capitals and punctuation in the following sentences as needed.

1. turn up the tv said her mother dont you want to hear the news

2. hank aaron broke babe ruths home run record in april 1974

3. the daily news is published at 220 e 42 st new york n y

4. gen eisenhower became president of the usa

5. dr john f sawyer has office hours from 9 am to 2 pm on mondays and fridays

6. oh dear i forgot to buy lettuce eggs and milk

7. mr tribuno my boss called me into the managers office

8. this was his order screws bolts nuts nails washers

9. its such a mess i cant stand it

10. the childrens toys and the boys bicycles are all over the yard

11. shouldnt the cat eat its dinner

12. john please pass the butter said his father

13. sir i admit your general rule

that every poet is a fool

but you yourself may serve to show it

that every fool is not a poet

Samuel Taylor Coleridge

14. hear me o lord when i cry unto thee

15. columbus discovered america on oct 12 1492

Answer Key for Diagnostic Test

I.

1. The <u>boy</u> yelled.

2. Dark threatening <u>clouds</u> gathered over-head.

3. <u>Joe</u> and <u>Tony</u> played catch.

4. <u>I</u> went to the grocery store.

5. In the dark sky shone the bright <u>stars</u>.

6. An <u>eagle</u> soared over the lake.

7. <u>Chicago</u> is in Illinois.

8. <u>Julie</u> washed the dishes and <u>Betsy</u> dried them.

---

1. Why does *an* (and not *a*) come before *eagle* in sentence 6? *"An" is used before words that begin with a vowel.*

2. Each subject in the above sentences (except in sentence 4) is the name of a person, place, or thing. What is the grammatical term for such a word? *Noun.*

3. What is the grammatical term for the word "I" in sentence 4? *Pronoun*

---

4. In sentence 2, find the simple subject and write it here. *Clouds*

5. Write the complete subject of sentence 2 here. *Dark threatening clouds.*

6. Find a compound subject in one of the preceding sentences and write it here.

   Joe and Tony

7. Find the subjects of a compound sentence and write them here. *Julie, Betsy*

II.

1. <u>Birds</u>|fly.
   - S | P

2. The <u>team</u>|played hard.
   - S | P

3. The <u>crowd</u>|shouted and cheered.
   - S | P

4. <u>Maria</u>|is the oldest <u>woman</u> in the <u>office</u>.
   - S | P

5. Overhead roared|a jet <u>plane</u>.
   - P | S

6. The <u>day</u>|was bright and sunny.
   - S | P

7. In the <u>distance</u> we|heard the <u>band</u>.
   - S | P

8. <u>Charlie</u>|threw <u>Jim</u> a fast <u>ball</u>.
   - S | P

9. I am the best pitcher on the team.
   (S) (P)

10. The boys/fought and kicked the intrud-
    (S) (P)
    er.

III.

1. Draw a line under every noun in the sentences above. How many did you find? __17__

2. Find an example of a common noun in sentence 6. __day__

3. Find proper nouns in sentences 4 and 8. __Maria, Charlie, Jim.__

4. Find a plural noun. __birds, boys.__

5. Find a singular noun in sentence 9. __pitcher.__

6. Find a collective noun in sentence 3. __crowd.__

7. Find a predicate noun in sentence 4. __woman__

8. Find the noun that is the direct object in sentence 10. __intruder__

9. Find a noun that is the indirect object in sentence 8. __Jim__

10. Write the plural or singular form of the following nouns.

    wolf __wolves__

story	__stories__	
radio	__radios__	
key	__keys__	
hero	__heroes__	
__wife__		wives
__mouse__		mice
__ox__		oxen
__tooth__		teeth
__sheep__		sheep

IV.

1. The caged lion roared fiercely.

2. It is a beautiful day.

3. High in the treetop the bird sings.

4. We were late to work.

5. All night long the baby cried.

1. Give an example of a verb expressing action in the past.
   __roared, cried.__

2. Give an example of a verb expressing action in the present.
   __sings.__

3. Give an example of a verb expressing being in the past.
   __were.__

4. Give an example of a verb expressing being in the present. __is.__

5. Give the present or past tense of the following irregular verbs.

~~ring~~	~~fought~~
~~take~~	~~told~~
~~win~~	~~drank~~
~~write~~	~~fed~~
~~shoot~~	~~fell~~

V.

1. <u>She</u> went to the movies with <u>me</u>.

2. <u>We</u> took <u>them</u> to the ball game.

3. He and I are good friends with them.

4. <u>You</u> can come with <u>us</u> to visit <u>him</u>.

5. They put <u>her</u> on the stretcher.

SUBJECTS	OBJECTS
She	*me*
We	*them*
He	*us*
I	*him*
You	*her*
They	

VI.

1. The fat little boy ran down the dusty street.

2. That tall blonde girl is the smartest in the whole senior class.

3. She certainly is intelligent!

1. In the above sentences find an adjective in the predicate that describes the subject. *smartest, intelligent.*

2. Give the comparative forms of the adjective "little." *littler, littlest*

3. Give the comparative forms of "intelligent." *more intelligent, most intelligent*

VII.

1. Slowly and painfully he hobbled up the mountain.

2. The beautifully decorated room was very impressive to me.

3. Very quietly he walked down the steps.

1.

slow	*beautiful*
painful	*quiet*

2. *adjective*

3. *adverb*

4. *adverb*

5. *adjective*

VIII.

PREPOSITIONS	OBJECTS
up	*mountain*
to	*me*
down	*steps*

IX.   1. <u>Oh, darn!</u> I hooked it, (but) it got away!

2. <u>Hey</u>, wait for Tony (and) me.

3. <u>Wow</u>, did you see that?

4. I'm late (because) I got lost.

X.   Sentence 1 *Exclamation*

Sentence 2 *Command*

Sentence 3 *Question*

Sentence 4 *Statement*

Every sentence must express a complete thought. Draw a line through any incomplete sentences below. Separate run-on sentences by using the proper punctuation.

1. First he shined his shoes. Then he took a shower.

2. ~~Opening the window and shouting at him.~~

3. He put a sinker on the line. It sank into the water.

4. ~~As soon as breakfast was over.~~

XI.   1. "Turn up the TV," said her mother, "don't you want to hear the news?"

2. Hank Aaron broke Babe Ruth's home run record in April, 1974.

3. <u>The Daily News</u> is published at 220 E. 42 St., New York N.Y.

4. Gen. Eisenhower became president of the USA.

5. Dr. John F. Sawyer has office hours from 9 AM to 2 PM on Mondays and Fridays.

6. Oh dear, I forgot to buy lettuce, eggs, and milk.

7. Mr. Tribuno, my boss, called me into the manager's office.

8. This was his order: screws, bolts, nuts, nails, washers.

9. It's such a mess I can't stand it!

10. The children's toys and the boys' bicycles are all over the yard.

11. Shouldn't the cat eat its dinner?

12. "John, please pass the butter," said his father

13. Sir, I admit your general rule,
That every poet is a fool,
But you yourself may serve to show it,
That every fool is not a poet.

Samuel Taylor Coleridge

14. Hear me, O Lord, when I cry unto thee.

15. Columbus discovered America on Oct. 12, 1492.

Chapter 1

Subjects and Predicates

In English every sentence must have two parts: a *subject* and a *predicate*. The subject is the person or thing that performs some action; the predicate tells what the subject does.

Example

Dogs bark.

Here *dogs* is the subject which performs the action, and *bark* is the predicate, which tells what dogs do. Words such as *dogs, men, fish, table,* or *ball* are called *nouns*. They are the *names* of people, places, or things. Nouns are the subjects of all the sentences below.

The words that express the action in a sentence—what the subject does—are called *verbs*. The verb is the main word in the predicate. It is usually the easiest word to find. In separating a sentence into its subject and predicate, always LOOK FOR THE ACTION. When you find it, ask yourself: "Who or what performed that action?" The answer to that question will help you find the subject.

Example

Guns shoot.

The action word or verb here is *shoot*. Draw two lines under it, and ask yourself who or what shoots? The answer is *guns*, which is a noun. Draw one line under it. You have now located the subject and the predicate. Draw a line between them and you have separated the basic parts of this sentence. Follow these three steps as you do Exercise 1.

Separating Subjects and Predicates

EXERCISE 1

First Step.

Look for the verb, the word that expresses action, and draw two lines under it.

Second Step.

Look for the name of the person or thing that performs the action and draw one line under it.

Third Step.

Draw a line between these two words to separate the subject from the predicate. Write *S* over the subject, *P* over the predicate.

Example

S   P
The <u>dog</u> / <u>barked</u>.

1. Fish swim.

2. Bees buzz.

3. Birds fly.

17

4. Babies cry.

5. Cats purr.

6. Trains run.

7. Planes fly.

8. Boats sail.

9. Wood burns.

10. Children play.

Notice that every sentence begins with a capital letter and ends with a period.

What you have just done is called "diagramming" a sentence. You have made a diagram of the main parts of the sentence. Now turn to the key of correct answers at the end of the book and go over your work. If you had no errors, you are ready to go on to Exercise 2. Always check your work after each exercise. If you make mistakes, go back and read the instructions again—until you are sure you understand them and know why you made errors.

In Exercise 2 you will notice that the sentences are longer. There may be more words than just the noun in the subject or just the verb in the predicate. We will learn about them later. Follow the same three steps as you diagram the sentences in Exercise 2.

EXERCISE 2

1. The snow fell.

2. A flower bloomed.

3. The girl cried.

4. The food smelled good.

5. A boy yelled.

6. The car speeds by.

7. The man whistled softly.

8. A girl laughed.

9. The bells rang loudly.

10. The clock struck ten.

Nouns as Subjects

Nouns are names. They are the names of people, places, or things. Words like *house, dog, tree, man, Washington, apple,* or *Saturday* are all nouns. Most nouns are preceded by *the* or *a,* but if a noun begins with a vowel sound (*a, e, i, o,* or *u*) it is preceded by *an.*

Examples

The man
A dog
An apple
The house
A tree
An umbrella
A shoe
The store
An idiot
The truth

We have seen that nouns are very important because they tell who or what is doing something. Every sentence must contain a noun which is the *subject* of the sentence. The subject is the person or thing which is performing the action.

Finding Subjects

EXERCISE 3

In the following exercise, draw a line under the subject of each sentence. If you have trouble, LOOK FOR THE ACTION! Then ask yourself who or what performed the action. Who played in sentence 1? What barked in sentence 2?

1. The boys played baseball.

2. A dog barked far away.

3. The car speeded past.

4. A policeman stopped it.

5. The driver looked unhappy.

6. The ticket cost him ten dollars.

7. An apple rolled off the table.

8. The women shopped for bargains.

9. Jimmy loves to fish.

10. An eagle soared across the sky.

Now look at the words you have underlined. Each one names people or things which are doing something. They are the subjects of the action taking place in the sentence.

Notice also that most of the nouns are preceded by *the* or *a*. *The* refers to certain definite subjects (e.g., the driver, the women); *a* or *an* refers to indefinite, nonspecific subjects. *A dog* is one of many dogs (see sentence 2), but *the boys* (sentence 1) refers to a specific group of boys. *An* is used before the two nouns, *apple* and *eagle*, which begin with vowels (*a, e, i, o,* or *u*). All other letters, all the hard sounds such as *d, t, k,* or *b,* are called consonants and are preceded by *a.*

EXERCISE 4

Draw a line under each subject.

1. The clouds gathered in the east.

2. A plane roared overhead.

3. The flowers wilted without water.

4. The telephone rang for a long time.

5. An ostrich has long legs.

6. The traffic grew much heavier.

7. Alice danced around the room.

8. An umbrella keeps off the rain.

9. The students did their homework.

10. A lady wrote to her son.

Check your answer key carefully. Did you find all the subjects? How many subjects were preceded by *a*?____ How many by *an*?____ Write the vowels at the beginnings of the words preceded by *an.*_____

Making up Subjects

EXERCISE 5

Make up your own subjects for the following incomplete sentences, and write them in the blank spaces. Be sure that the first word begins with a capital. Your subject must be a noun which refers to the person or thing performing the action described in the rest of the sentence.

When you have finished, diagram the completed sentence by underlining the verb twice, the subject once, and drawing a line between the subject and the predicate.

Example
_____ / ran down the street.
You might write in as subjects:
A dog
The thief

1._____ walked into the pizza parlor.

2._____ handed out hundred dollar bills.

3._____ growled furiously outside the door.

4._____ chased the frightened child.

5._____ sits under a tree and dreams.

6._____ drove a big blue Cadillac.

7._____ dug deep into the soft earth.

8._____ wore a crazy flowered hat.

9. _____ stalked across the empty stage.

10. _____ shouted angrily at the boy.

When you have finished, count how many of the subjects you wrote down are preceded by *the*. Record the number below. Then count how many are preceded by *a*. Make sure you have not used *a* before a word that begins with a vowel (*a, e, i, o,* or *u*). Write below the number of subjects preceded by *the*, by *a*, or by *an*.

The	A	An
_____	_____	_____

Verbs as Predicates

We have learned that it is not possible to construct a sensible sentence without having a noun which is the subject. In the same way, every sentence must also have a *verb* which tells what the subject does. Just as a locomotive pulls a train or an engine drives a car, so a verb supplies the action in a sentence.

Examples

Judy dances.
The dog barked.

We have seen that the part of the sentence which contains the verb is called the *predicate*. There may be more words than just the verb in the predicate.

Example

The dog/barked fiercely during the night.

Here the predicate contains not only the verb *barked* but also the word *fiercely* which tells *how* the dog barked and the phrase *during the night* which tells *when* the dog barked.

In the same way, the subject may also have words which describe or *modify* it, although the main subject can only be the noun which is the doer of the action expressed by the verb.

Example

Subject   Predicate
The huge, ferocious dog/barked loudly.

In this sentence the *dog* is the doer; the other words describe or *modify* the *dog*. The verb is *barked*, although the complete predicate is *barked loudly*. The word *loudly* modifies the verb; it tells *how* the dog barked.

EXERCISE 6

Diagram the following sentences by underlining the verb twice, the subject once, and drawing a line between the subject and the complete predicate.

1. The boy dialed the wrong number.

2. The painter fell off the ladder.

3. The chef prepares a delicious meal.

4. The family ate dinner at the new restaurant.

5. A dog chases a squirrel in the park.

6. An artist drew a sketch of the old bridge.

7. The elephant escapes from the zoo.

8. An apple falls from the tree.

9. The dentist filled the cavity quickly.

10. The elevator stopped on the tenth floor.

When you diagram a sentence you map out its framework so that it becomes easy to see how the sentence is constructed. After you have checked your work with the answer key, read aloud the words you have underlined above. See how the main words in the sentence jump out at you so that you can easily see its basic structure. The other words, which we will study later, are all window dressing for the noun and verb which you have underlined.

Making up the Predicate

EXERCISE 7

Make up a predicate for each of the following

subjects and diagram the sentence as usual. Be sure you think of a verb which expresses some action the subject might be performing.

1. The hairy monster _____.

2. An astronaut _____.

3. The fat old lady _____.

4. A green sports car _____.

5. The husky policeman _____.

6. My grandmother _____.

7. The tall waiter _____.

8. The girl's blond hair _____.

9. The frightened horse _____.

10. The baseball team _____.

Review of Diagraming

EXERCISE 8

Every sentence must have:
1. A subject which performs the action. It is called a _____.
2. A predicate which describes the action the subject does. The main word is a _____.

Draw two lines under the verb or the word that expresses action. Then ask yourself who or what did this action? Find the *one* word that answers your question and draw a line under it. Draw a line between the noun and the verb and write *S* over the subject and *P* over the predicate.

1. Frank whistled.

2. The birds sang.

3. The employees ate lunch.

4. Our team won.

5. Mary fed her cat.

6. Joe dropped his hammer.

7. The clock stopped.

8. A bell rang.

9. The sun shone in the sky.

10. Flowers blossom in spring.

11. The moon rose across the lake.

12. The canoe glided down the river.

13. The red car roared down the street.

14. Ed hit the ball hard.

15. The boys played a game.

16. The passengers lined up quickly.

17. The supervisor handed out the paychecks.

18. The big black dog chased me away.

19. The goldfish swims around the pond.

20. The shining stars gleam in the sky.

Give yourself 5 points for each sentence you diagramed correctly. Take off 3 points for each error. What is your score? If it is 80 or more, go on to the next section. If it is lower than 80, go back and review what we have covered. Be sure you understand your mistakes before going on.

Simple and Complete Predicates

EXERCISE 9

We have already seen that the verb is the main word in the predicate, but not always the only word. Sometimes the predicate is a group of words.

Example
S   P——————————————→
The <u>dog</u> / <u>barked</u> loudly at the boys.

In this case the verb is called the *simple predicate,* while the whole group of words, *barked loudly at the boys,* forms the *complete predicate.*

In the following sentences, locate the verb or simple predicate which describes the action and draw two lines under it. Then find the name of the subject that performs that action and draw one line under it. Write *S* over the subject, *P* over the verb or simple predicate, and separate them with a line. Draw arrows to show the complete predicate.

1. Fish swim all over the lake.

2. Bees buzz around the flowers all day.

3. Birds fly south in the winter.

4. Babies cry when they are hungry.

5. Cats purr deep down in their throats.

6. Trains run from Boston to California.

7. Planes fly very low over the airport.

8. Boats sail up and down the lake.

9. Plants need sunlight and water.

10. Children play in the park.

Stop and correct your work from the answer key before going on to Exercise 10. You will notice that in Exercise 9 all the subjects consist of only one word, while the complete predicates are quite long. In Exercise 10 the complete subject may contain other words which describe or *modify* the noun which is the subject. Diagram these sentences as you did in Exercise 9.

EXERCISE 10

1. The snow fell three feet deep last night.

2. A red flower bloomed in her garden.

3. The girl cried because she couldn't go.

4. The food smelled good to the hungry men.

5. A boy yelled at the big bully.

6. The foreign car speeds by with the police after it.

7. The man whistled softly to himself.

8. A girl laughed at his joke.

9. The church bells rang loudly on Sunday morning.

10. The clock struck ten in the empty old house.

Simple and Complete Subjects

EXERCISE 11

The subject, like the predicate, may be a group of words or a *phrase.* After you have located and underlined the *verb* or simple predicate twice, ask yourself: "Who or what performed this action?" Then underline once the *one* word which is the subject or the doer of that action. That word is called the *simple subject.* It is a *noun* which names the person or thing performing the action. The other words simply describe or tell you more about that noun, just as *big* and *yellow* describe the subject *dog* below.

Example

$$\longleftarrow \qquad\quad \overset{S}{\underline{}} \; \overset{P}{\underline{}} \longrightarrow$$

The big yellow dog/barked loudly at the strangers.

In the following sentences, locate and underline the simple predicate or verb twice and the simple subject or noun once. Then separate and label the subject and predicate with arrows to show what words are included in the complete subject and complete predicate.

1. The big gray cat sat on the fence.

2. Thick white snowflakes drifted down.

3. A very tall boy ran across the street.

4. A big red car roared down the highway.

5. A police car speeded after it.

6. A fat old lady rocked the baby.

7. The shouting boys skated in the park.

8. A sleepy old man opened the door.

9. Two tired children crawled into bed.

10. The red-headed girl spells very well.

EXERCISE 12

You may have noticed by now that, although the simple subject is always a noun, not every noun is a subject. In Exercise 12, look at sentences 2, 3, 5, 7, 8, and 10. See how many nouns you can find in the predicate and list them below, after you have diagramed the sentences as you did in Exercise 11.

_____ _____

_____ _____

_____ _____

_____ _____

1. The young actor combed his hair.

2. My sister answered the telephone.

3. Our football team beat the other team.

4. Our coach praised our good playing.

5. The silent thief sneaked into the house.

6. The big watchdog barked at him.

7. A policeman drove his car up the street.

8. The sneaky thief ran away from the dog.

9. The policeman grabbed him as he ran.

10. The watchdog became the hero of the day.

Compound Subjects and Predicates

When a sentence has more than one subject for the same verb it is called a *compound subject*.

Example
> Judy and Nancy / shopped in the department store.

When a sentence has more than one verb with the same subject it is called a *compound predicate* or a *compound verb*.

Example
> The audience / laughed and applauded.

EXERCISE 13

Find subjects and predicates in the following sentences, underlining and separating them as usual. If there is a compound subject write CS above it. If there is a compound predicate write CP above it.

Example

C P
The dog / leaped and jumped.

C S
The men and women / crowded into the subway.

1. Rachel and Bill took a taxi home.

2. The audience cheers and claps for the actor.

3. Mike, Tom, and Betsy organized the meeting.

4. The young man slips and falls on the ice.

5. The car and the bike collided at the light.

6. The guests laugh and dance at the party.

7. Nancy and her sister left early.

8. They bought groceries and cooked dinner.

9. Mary opened the door and walked into the room.

10. Steve and his girl friend had an argument.

How many compound subjects did you find?____

How many compound predicates did you find?__

EXERCISE 14

Write sentences using the following *compound subjects:*

1. Beth and Jane_____.

2. Ships and airplanes_____.

3. Dogs and cats_____.

4. Thunder and lightning_____.

5. Men and women_____.

Write sentences using the following *compound predicates:*

1. _____ danced and sang.

2. _____ run and jump.

3. _____ struggled and sweated.

4. _____ told jokes and played games.

5. _____ jumped into the water and swam.

Review Test of Subjects and Predicates

In the following sentences, locate and underline the simple predicate or verb twice and the simple subject or noun once. Separate and draw arrows over the complete subject and predicate. Label compound subjects *CS* and compound predicates *CP*.

EXERCISE 15

1. The frightened kitten crawled under the bed.

2. The cross old lady scolded the waiter.

3. Torn yellow curtains hung in the window.

4. The winter wind shrieked and howled down the alley.

5. Robins and bluejays sat in a tree.

6. The excited brown puppy ran around barking.

7. A beautiful girl bought the white satin dress.

8. The fat little boy and his brother ate the whole cake.

9. A train whistled loudly.

10. The train roared into the station.

11. The shining moon rose over the city.

12. A cherry tree bloomed in the park.

13. The winter rain poured down on the earth.

14. The thin man hurried down the street.

15. The angry dogs growled and barked at the stranger.

16. The hungry fish swim toward the bait.

17. The warm spring sun shone brightly.

18. The red sports car roared up the hill.

19. The very exciting game ended finally.

20. The noisy boys shouted and cheered.

Give yourself 5 points for each correctly diagramed sentence. Take off 2 points for each error. Did you score over 80? If so, go on to the next chapter after correcting your mistakes. If your score is less than 80, go back and reread the instructions; then do the exercises again. It is important that you understand each step before going on.

Chapter 2

More About Nouns

We have said that a noun is usually the name of a person, place, or thing. Sometimes it is a time, like *midnight*; or a season, like *autumn*; or an idea, like *democracy*. So far we have been looking at nouns only as subjects; but we have seen that sometimes there are other nouns in the sentences we have studied. A noun can be not only the *doer* of the verb's action, but it can also receive the action. In that case it is called the *object* of the action or the *object* of the verb.

Examples

SUBJECT	VERB	OBJECT
Jim	hit	Bill.
The boy	ate	the apple.
A dog	bit	the man.

In these sentences the action begins in the subject and ends in the object. The apple did not eat the boy, and Bill did not start the fight. The *object* answers the question "Who or what?" Jim hit (whom?). The boy ate (what?). A dog bit (what?). The noun which receives the action is called the *object of the verb*.

EXERCISE 16

Diagram the following sentences and label the parts *S* for the subject, *P* for the verb or simple predicate, and *O* for the object.

Example
```
              S      P    O
         Babies / drink milk.
```

1. The cat chased a mouse.

2. His mother called Tom.

3. My sister wore my dress.

4. The policeman grabbed the thief.

5. The firemen stopped the fire.

6. His car hit a tree.

7. The teacher graded the papers.

8. The mother rocked the baby.

9. The man paid his bill.

10. The wind rattles the windows.

Now stop and correct these sentences before going on to the harder ones in Exercise 17. Did you find the objects of action in each sentence?

EXERCISE 17

1. The dog gnawed his bone.

2. A bird sang a song.

3. The farmer planted seed.

4. Snow covered the ground.

5. The ship hit a reef.

6. The waves pounded the rocks.

7. A jet plane broke the sound barrier.

8. The capsule hit the ocean.

9. The rocket missed its target.

10. A bomb shattered the building.

Proper Nouns and Common Nouns

You have noticed that some nouns begin with capital letters and some do not. Nouns that refer to particular persons, places, or things are called *proper nouns*. They begin with capital letters. Ordinary nouns which refer to any one of a class of persons, places, or things are called *common nouns*. They do *not* begin with capital letters. For example, if you were writing about rivers in general, *rivers* would be a *common noun*. But if you were referring to the *Hudson River* you would begin with capitals because that is the name of a particular river. A proper noun always begins with a capital and is the name of a particular person, place, or thing. As you have seen, proper nouns sometimes contain more than one word: *Hudson River* or *Casey Stengel*.

In the following sentences, put a circle around each proper noun and an *X* above each common noun. Remember that the first word in a sentence has a capital but it may not be a proper noun.

Example

X
The (President) and his family live in the (White House.)

EXERCISE 18

1. Julie asked her mother for a quarter.

2. The fish swam around the pond.

3. Jonah was swallowed by a whale.

4. The little yellow bird sang in the tree.

5. June is my favorite month.

6. Robert moved to California.

7. His father bought a house in Los Angeles.

8. The picture fell off the wall.

9. Mary asked Grandmother to read her a story.

10. The dog bit the mailman.

Did you find 8 proper nouns, beginning with capitals? Did you find 15 common nouns? Check the answer key.

EXERCISE 19

1. Patty has a brother named David.

2. A little white rabbit ran across the yard.

3. Central Park is in New York.

4. Mary answered the telephone.

5. The children were going to school.

6. Don plays for the Mets.

7. Abe hit the ball with a stick.

8. The cheerful cook baked a big chocolate cake for Christmas Day.

9. My favorite sports are football, tennis, and track.

10. George, Joe, and Tony have parts in a show on Broadway.

Singular and Plural Nouns

Nouns may be singular or plural.

Singular nouns refer to one of anything.
  a boy
  the cat
  an apple

Plural nouns refer to more than one. They usually end in *s* or *es*.
  some boys
  the three cats
  a dozen apples

EXERCISE 20

Put a circle around each proper noun and an *X* above each common noun in the following sentences. Put an *S* over each singular noun and a *P* over each plural noun.

Example

           S
The (Empire State Building) has over a
           XP
hundred stories.

1. The girl bought a hat in the store.

2. The families of the Canadians waited at the airport.

3. The boys played ball with Billy.

4. My home is in Chicago, but I have a bungalow on Lake Erie.

5. Betty dropped a dish on the floor of the restaurant.

6. My cat chased Fido across the grass and down Elm Street.

7. On Sunday the fellows went to Shea Stadium.

8. The wolves howl on the mountains on cold winter nights.

9. John and his brother assembled the Volkswagen.

10. Those boys belong to Little League.

Did you find 20 common nouns? Did you find 12 proper nouns? Did you find 24 singular nouns? Did you find 7 plural nouns? Remember that every sentence begins with a capital, so not every word with a capital is a proper noun.

EXERCISE 21

Put a circle around each proper noun and an *X* above each common noun in the following sentences. Mark singulars and plurals with S or P.

1. George Washington was our first president.

2. Mark Twain and Washington Irving are famous American writers.

3. The Amazon is the longest river in South America.

4. The Giants won the game with the Jets last Saturday.

5. Sons often grow up to be like their fathers.

6. There are many pink flowers on the cherry tree.

7. One tulip bloomed in my garden.

8. Jupiter is a planet with several moons.

9. Venus and Mars are also planets.

10. We had beef and potatoes for dinner.

Irregular Plurals

The plural of nouns ending in *y* which have a vowel (*a, e, i, o,* or *u*) before the *y* is formed by adding *s*.

Examples

        boy   boys
        day   days

Nouns ending in *y* which do not have a vowel (*a, e, i, o,* or *u*) before the *y* form the plural by changing the *y* to *i* and then adding *es.*

Examples

        baby   babies
        cry   cries

EXERCISE 22

Form the plurals of these words ending in *y.*

1. toy   _____

2. body   _____

3. guy   _____

4. lady   _____

5. fly   _____

6. party   _____

7. sky   _____

8. key   _____

9. hobby   _____

10. story   _____

EXERCISE 23

Do you need more practice? Try these, looking at each one to see whether a vowel (*a, e, i, o,* or *u*) precedes the final *y.*

1. chimney   _____

2. company   _____

3. valley   _____

4. pony   _____

5. ray   _____

6. bunny   _____

7. family   _____

8. delay   _____

9. monkey   _____

10. candy   _____

The same rules apply to words ending in *o.* If the *o* is preceded by a vowel, the plural is formed just by adding *s.*

Examples

        radio   radios
        zoo   zoos

But words that end in *o* not preceded by a vowel form the plural by adding *es.*

Examples

        hero   heroes
        potato   potatoes

There are some exceptions to these rules, chiefly musical terms and musical instruments, where the plural is formed just by adding *s.*

Examples

        banjo   banjos
        solo   solos

EXERCISE 24

Form the plurals of the following words; use a dictionary if you are not sure.

PLURAL		SINGULAR	PLURAL
1. trio	_____	mouse	mice
		child	children
2. tomato	_____	man	men
		woman	women
3. rodeo	_____	foot	feet
		goose	geese
4. piano	_____	ox	oxen
		tooth	teeth
5. photo	_____	louse	lice
		postman	postmen
6. igloo	_____		

The singular and plural forms of some nouns are the same.

7. embargo _____

8. auto _____

Examples

9. cargo _____

sheep	moose
deer	trout
swine	bass

10. hero _____

Some words ending in *f* or *fe* change the *f* to *v* before adding the plural.

Collective Nouns

Examples

EXERCISE 25

leaf	leaves
wife	wives

Some nouns use the singular form to refer to a number of people or things. They are called *collective nouns* because they refer to a collection or a group.

Learn the words in the examples and in the list below. You will then know most of the exceptions which form their plurals in this way.

Examples

SINGULAR	PLURAL
life	lives
elf	elves
loaf	loaves
calf	calves
shelf	shelves
thief	thieves
wolf	wolves
self	selves
sheaf	sheaves
half	halves
knife	knives

An <u>audience</u> of listeners
A <u>group</u> of people
A <u>troop</u> of Boy Scouts
An <u>army</u> of soldiers
A <u>flock</u> of birds
A <u>herd</u> of sheep
A <u>grove</u> of trees
A church <u>congregation</u>

Some nouns have completely different forms in the plural. These are called *irregular nouns.* You will just have to memorize these, or look them up in the dictionary, since there is no rule which governs their spelling.

Write the proper collective noun on the line.

1. A_____ of cows grazed in the meadow.

2. A_____ of chickens was in the yard.

3. A_____of children played in the park.

4. The United States_____trains its officers at West Point.

5. The_____in the theater enjoyed the show.

6. The_____of the church attended Sunday services.

7. A_____of boys gathered on the street.

8. A_____of pine trees grew in the valley.

9. Our baseball _____ won the game.

10. My Boy Scout_____went on a hike.

12. tomatoes _____

13. teeth _____

14. cabbages _____

15. horses _____

16. hobbies _____

17. lice _____

18. knives _____

19. knees _____

20. laces _____

Review of Singular and Plural Nouns

EXERCISE 26

For the plural nouns below, write their singular forms in the space provided.

PLURAL	SINGULAR
1. thieves	_____
2. women	_____
3. houses	_____
4. mice	_____
5. armies	_____
6. nations	_____
7. pianos	_____
8. boxes	_____
9. children	_____
10. nurses	_____
11. leaves	_____

Review Test of Nouns

EXERCISE 27

A noun is the name of a_____,

_____, or _____ .

Nouns may be
1) common or proper.
2) singular or plural.
3) subject or object of the verb.

Diagram the following sentences as usual and circle the direct object if there is one.

Example
The boys / chased the (dog) down the street.

Always read back to yourself the marked words to see if they make sense. *Boys chased dog* expresses a complete thought and contains the sense of the sentence. *Boys chased street* does not make sense. In this case the noun *street* tells *where* the boys chased, not *what* they chased. The *dog* is the object because the dog received the action of being chased in the sentence.

1. Sally wears slacks to work.

2. The bird carried a worm to its nest.

3. Frank and Mario raced their cars down the highway.

4. A policeman drove his motorcycle after them.

5. The tall trooper gave a ticket to each of them.

6. A flock of ducks waddled across the road.

7. Sandy and Liz enjoyed the movie.

8. The children jumped and ran in the playground.

9. The sun rose from behind the mountains.

10. The American army won the battle.

Find examples of the following in the sentences above and write them in the spaces provided:

PROPER NOUNS	COMMON NOUNS
_____	_____
_____	_____
_____	_____
_____	_____
_____	_____

SINGULAR NOUNS	PLURAL NOUNS
_____	_____
_____	_____
_____	_____

_____   _____

_____   _____

Explain the following terms:

1. A compound subject_____

_____.

2. A compound predicate_____

_____.

3. A collective noun_____

_____.

Diagram the following sentences as usual. Put a circle around any objects.

1. A robin built its nest in the tree.

2. The Bermans and the Shaws live in Chicago.

3. Julie and Pam led the parade.

4. The crowd shouted and screamed.

5. Our team won three football games.

6. A gang of boys broke windows in the school.

7. A policeman caught and arrested the fellows.

8. Our club elected a president named Joe Ferrara.

9. The astronauts walked in outer space.

10. The rocket reached the moon safely.

Fill the spaces below with examples of each of the following:

COMPOUND
SUBJECT

_____

_____

COMPOUND PREDICATE

_____

_____

COLLECTIVE NOUNS

_____

_____

Find examples of the following nouns. (You may use the same noun more than once if you wish.)

PROPER	COMMON	SINGULAR	PLURAL
_____	_____	_____	_____
_____	_____	_____	_____
_____	_____	_____	_____
_____	_____	_____	_____
_____	_____	_____	_____

Give yourself 3 points for each correct sentence and 1 point for each space correctly filled. Take off 1 point for each mistake. If you are careful, you could get more than 100!

Chapter 3

Pronouns

Pronouns are little words that stand for nouns, just as movie stars have stand-ins. They always refer back to a previous noun; otherwise they make no sense.

Example

He took it to him.

This sentence has no meaning unless you know what the pronouns *he*, *it*, and *him* refer to.

Example

Bill's father asked Bill for the newspaper. He (Bill) took it (the paper) to him (Bill's father).

Pronouns are useful because they save us from a lot of tiresome repetition of the same words.

Example

Carl and Maria and Joe were late to work so they (Carl and Maria and Joe) reported to their boss. They (Carl and Maria and Joe) told him (the boss) that their (Carl's and Maria's and Joe's) subway had lost power and made them (Carl and Maria and Joe) late to work.

Pronouns are different from nouns because they change in form when they become objects.

Example

He (subject) called him (object).

The only pronouns that do not change in form are *you* and *it*. The forms of the others are given below.

SUBJECT	OBJECT	EXAMPLE
I	me	She likes me.
he	him	I like him.
she	her	He likes her.
we	us	They like us.
they	them	We like them.

EXERCISE 28

In each of the following sentences fill in the blank with the correct form of the pronoun, depending on whether it is a subject or an object.

1. Bill chased_____into the house. (I, me)

2. _____began to scream for my mother. (I, Me)

3. _____came running when she heard. (She, Her)

4. Joe and Harry came home for dinner with _____ . (I, me)

33

5. My mother cooked a turkey for_____.
   (they, them)

6. After dinner_____all watched TV.
   (we, us)

7. Do you want to come with_____?
   (we, us)

8. _____are going to a show. (We, Us)

9. _____was wearing a new dress.
   (She, Her)

10. It looked beautiful on_____. (she, her)

You will note that in the above sentences there are little words such as *with, for,* and *on* which are followed by nouns ("for my mother" in sentence 2) or pronouns ("with me" in sentence 4). These little words are called *prepositions* and will be discussed later. They take nouns or pronouns as objects. So we say "with me," not "with I."

In Exercise 29, there are four prepositions, *to, with, between,* and *among,* which are also followed by objects.

When two pronouns are used in a compound subject, as in sentence 6, Exercise 29, it is polite usage always to refer to yourself last. The same rule applies to compound objects. Be careful to use the correct form of the pronoun, depending on whether it is a subject or an object.

Examples

My buddy and *I* (not *me*) went bowling.

The dog chased Eddie and *me* (not *I*).

Review Test of Pronouns

EXERCISE 29

In each of the following sentences fill in the blank with the correct form of the pronoun, depending on whether it is a subject or an object.

1. Polly and_____went swimming. (I, me)

2. _____ and Mary went to the movies.
   (He, Him)

3. They went with my boy friend and_____.
   (I, me)

4. Either Dan or_____will pick you up.
   (I, me)

5. You can go with_____if you want.
   (we, us)

6. _____and_____are buddies.
   (He, Him; I, me)

7. That's secret between you and_____.
   (I, me)

8. They have an agreement among_____.
   (they, them)

9. Both_____and_____were late to school. (she, her; I, me)

10. Was there a quarrel between_____
    (she, her) and_____? (he, him)

Chapter 4

More About Verbs

We have said that verbs supply the action in a sentence, that they tell what it is the subject does. An action verb is like the engine that makes the train run; the verb makes the subject run, or perform in some way.

Verbs also tell at what time an action takes place. Verbs have different forms to express different times. These time forms are called *tenses*. There are three main tenses in English—*present, past,* and *future*. When the action is happening now, the verb is in the *present* tense.

Examples
>I work hard on my job.
>I hate to leave my girl friend.

When the action happened in the past, the verb is in the *past* tense. This is usually formed by adding *d* or *ed* to the verb.

Examples
>I worked hard on my job.
>I hated to leave my girl friend.

Actions in the future are formed by adding *will* to the verb.

Examples
>I will work hard on my job.
>I will hate to leave my girl friend.

In this case the verb is more than one word and is called a *verb phrase*. There are many helping words such as *have* or *should* or *might* that are used to express various times and shades of meaning.

Examples
>I should have gone home.
>Marie might have called me.
>He had had a terrible experience.

We will not take up these more difficult forms of verbs in this book except to call them *verb phrases*. In such phrases the helping words change the meaning of the verb in some way. Thus, *will go* and *ought to go* do not mean the same as *go*.

Present and Past Tenses

EXERCISE 30

Form the past tense of the following verbs by adding *d* if the verb ends in *e* or *ed* if it does not. Words ending in *y* usually change the *y* to *i* before adding *ed*.

Examples

Present	Past
love	loved
fill	filled
try	tried

Say to yourself: "Today, I walk. Yesterday, I walked," etc.

PRESENT TENSE	PAST TENSE
1. skate	_____
2. study	_____
3. buzz	_____
4. bloom	_____
5. whistle	_____
6. light	_____
7. laugh	_____
8. cry	_____
9. marry	_____
10. wash	_____

EXERCISE 31

Write the present tense of each of the verbs given below in the space provided.

PRESENT TENSE	PAST TENSE
1. _____	wished
2. _____	asked
3. _____	liked
4. _____	tried
5. _____	dropped
6. _____	planted
7. _____	washed
8. _____	noted
9. _____	chased
10. _____	provided

EXERCISE 32

When we are speaking of another person or thing performing the action, the verb ends in *s* or *es*. Again, change the final *y* to *i* before adding the ending.

Examples

I run. He runs.
I cry. She cries.

Write the proper ending for the following verbs. Say to yourself: "He (she or it) raises."

1. raise	He	_____
2. dress	She	_____
3. hate	He	_____
4. brush	She	_____
5. fry	He	_____
6. smile	She	_____
7. want	He	_____
8. carry	She	_____
9. push	It	_____
10. wait	He	_____

Write the past tense of the following verbs. Say to yourself: "Today he (she or it) raises. Yesterday he raised."

1. raises	_____
2. dresses	_____
3. hates	_____
4. brushes	_____
5. fries	_____
6. smiles	_____

7. wants _____

8. pushes _____

9. waits _____

10. carries _____

EXERCISE 33

Write the present tense of each of the verbs given below in the space provided.

1. _____ He waited.

2. _____ It required.

3. _____ She rushed.

4. _____ He demanded.

5. _____ She cried.

6. _____ He screamed.

7. _____ It mated.

8. _____ He killed.

9. _____ It moved.

10. _____ He fired.

Irregular Verbs

EXERCISE 34

Many verbs in English change their forms when they change their tense.

Example
Today I ring the bell. Yesterday I rang the bell.

There are no rules for these verbs, which are called *irregular*. Many of them come to us from the language of the ancient Anglo-Saxons from which English is descended. The correct forms are usually learned when a child learns to talk. If you say each verb to yourself in sentences like the ones above, you can usually tell whether it sounds correct. If you aren't sure, look it up in a dictionary which gives the past tense.

Write the past tense of each verb given in the space provided. Be sure to say to yourself: "Today I_____. Yesterday I_____."

PRESENT	PAST
1. take	_____
2. run	_____
3. eat	_____
4. go	_____
5. come	_____
6. grow	_____
7. speak	_____
8. fight	_____
9. hit	_____
10. fall	_____
11. fly	_____
12. swim	_____
13. tell	_____
14. sing	_____
15. make	_____
16. rise	_____
17. shine	_____
18. win	_____
19. feed	_____
20. drink	_____

Make a list of any of these irregular forms you do not know and memorize them. Then try Exercise 35. Repeat these exercises until you are sure of all the irregular forms.

EXERCISE 35

Write the present tense of each of the following verbs in the space provided, making the subject another person. Say to yourself: "Yesterday he wrote. Today he writes."

1. _____ wrote

2. _____ won

3. _____ shot

4. _____ came

5. _____ went

6. _____ sat

7. _____ broke

8. _____ rose

9. _____ swam

10. _____ bought

11. _____ shone

12. _____ slept

13. _____ told

14. _____ lit

15. _____ caught

16. _____ bent

17. _____ fed

18. _____ held

19. _____ took

20. _____ thought

Verbs of Being

Verbs are not always *action* words. There are also verbs of *being,* the most common of which are *am, are, is, was,* and *were.* These verbs express no action, only a state of being. They are like equal signs in arithmetic.

Examples

Betsy is a girl.
Betsy = a girl.

I am your father.
I = your father.

Verbs of being are irregular. They change in form to agree with the subject. The subject may be a noun or a pronoun, the little word which acts as a stand-in for a noun.

PRESENT	PAST
I am	I was
You are	You were
He, she, or it is	He, she, or it was
We are	We were
You are	You were
They are	They were

EXERCISE 36

Diagram the following sentences in the usual way, with two lines under the verb of being, one line under the simple subject, and a vertical line separating the complete subject from the complete predicate. Label the two parts S or P.

Example S   P
The women / were late to work.

1. Celeste is a pretty girl.

2. The dog was black and white.

3. I am hungry for supper.

4. The men are outdoors.

5. The train was late tonight.

6. The stars were bright in the sky.

7. This horse is very smart.

8. The audience was too noisy.

9. I am glad to see my friend.

10. The women were in the office.

EXERCISE 37

Fill in a verb of being in each of the following sentences.

1. Richie_____the best pitcher.

2. Jim and Doug_____catchers on our team.

3. Julie Andrews_____the star in *Mary Poppins*.

4. At night I_____sleepy.

5. You think you_____so smart!

6. Yesterday you_____late to work.

7. Last summer Tim_____working.

8. Now he_____back in school.

9. This week my brother_____home on leave from the army.

10. Where_____you going tomorrow?

Pronouns with Verbs of Being

The most common verbs of being are *am, are, is, was,* and *were.* Memorize these five little

words because they are used very frequently. Verbs of being do not express action; they simply act like equal signs between the subject and the predicate. The predicate after a verb of being describes the subject or tells you something about it.

Examples
My name is Sue Jackson.
My name = Sue Jackson.

The boys are members of the team.
The boys = members of the team.

EXERCISE 38

Diagram the following sentences, but say to yourself: "Who or what is the subject?" instead of "Who or what does the action?"

1. She was very mean to me.

2. They are not nice to strangers.

3. Our family is together on weekends.

4. We were at the beach last Sunday.

5. The weather was very hot.

6. It was almost too hot to walk on the sand.

7. The waves were very powerful.

8. Sometimes people are not very thoughtful.

9. They were often at home.

10. I am pleased with your progress.

Find six pronoun subjects in the sentences above. Write them on the lines below.

1. _____   4. _____

2. _____   5. _____

3. _____   6. _____

EXERCISE 39

In the following sentences, write in the correct verb of being above the *equal* sign.

1. I = hungry.

2. He = my brother.

3. The boys = members of the baseball team.

4. Last year they = the high school champions.

5. She = the best student in the class.

6. We = very good friends.

7. We = watching TV at my house last night.

8. My mother = going out shopping.

9. Last year our coach = Chuck Wilson.

10. He = a very good coach all that year.

Verbs Preceding Their Subjects

EXERCISE 40

The subject of the sentence does not always come before the predicate. Sometimes the subject comes last in the sentence.

Always find the verb first. Then ask yourself who or what did the action or had being and you will find the subject.

Diagram the following sentences in the usual manner. After each sentence write *Pr* if it is in the present tense, *P* if it is in the past tense.

Example
In the east shone / a bright star.   P

1. In the last row sits John. _____

2. At the back of the room was a huge fireplace.

_____

3. Under my window grows a beautiful rose-bush._____

4. On the porch in a rocking chair sat the old, old lady._____

5. After all the cold weather comes the warm, lovely spring._____

6. Next to my house is a little park. _____

7. Down the chimney came Santa Claus!_____

8. After the dinner came a delicious dessert.____

9. Inside all the tissue paper was a tiny gold box.

_____

10. Last of all, after everybody else, came Peter!

_____

EXERCISE 41

In these sentences you may find the subject anywhere in the sentence. Diagram in the usual manner, marking S and P where needed. Circle any objects of verbs. You should find five objects.

1. Next to the wall the children planted flowers.

2. With great caution the robber opened the window.

3. Under the trees in the shade sat the old man.

4. With a terrible roar, the jet passed overhead.

5. After lunch the brothers went shopping.

6. Last of all comes the grand prize.

7. On Saturday we took a trip to Connecticut.

8. Barking angrily, the dog charged the stranger.

9. Smiling sweetly, the lady opened the door for the guests.

10. After the storm came the sunshine again.

Predicate Nouns

Verbs of being do not express action. Therefore they do not take objects, since no action is received. Nouns that follow a verb of being are called *predicate nouns*. They are simply another name for the subject.

Example

      Jim Grillo is my brother.

There is no action here. *Brother* is simply another name for *Jim Grillo*. Since it is in the predicate, it is called the *predicate noun*.

Example

      The boy ate the apple.

Remember that an object receives the action of the verb. In this sentence, *apple* is the object of the verb *ate*. For a review of objects, go back and do Exercise 16 again.

Diagram the following sentences in the usual manner and write *O* above the object. In sentences using verbs of being, write *PN* (predicate noun) above the noun in the predicate which describes or tells you something about the subject.

Examples

    S   P   O
John / kicked the football.
    S   P   PN
John / is the quarterback.

EXERCISE 42

1. The boys caught a fish.

2. My grandmother is Mrs. Wilson.

3. Jimmy hit a foul ball.

4. Mary is the oldest person here.

5. I am your new supervisor.

6. The boy slammed the door.

7. You are the last one to finish.

8. Joe carried the garbage can outside.

9. Tom shoveled the driveway for me.

10. The students did their work quickly.

How many predicate nouns did you find?

After a verb of being, a pronoun in the predicate is, like a noun, a *predicate pronoun*. In this case, the pronoun keeps the form of a subject.

Examples

      It is he who called me.
      It was they who started the fight.

The expression "It's me," while not correct in grammar, is widely used and is accepted nowadays. Actually, the correct expression would be "It's I," with the predicate pronoun *I* following the verb of being *is*.

EXERCISE 43

Follow the same directions as for Exercise 42.

1. John is a good friend of mine.

2. He opened the package from his sister.

3. Janet left her purse at home.

4. That desk is an antique.

5. We gave a party for the couple.

6. She is a reporter for the local newspaper.

7. They built their house themselves.

8. Bruce feeds his cat three times a day.

9. You are an excellent writer.

10. I am the best cook in my family.

Review of Verbs

Verbs that tell about what is happening now are

in the present time or *present tense*.

Verbs that tell what happened in the past are in the *past tense*. Most verbs form the past tense by adding *d* (as in poke*d*) or *ed* (as in sand*ed*).

Beside each verb below, write its past tense. Say to yourself: "Today I . . . . (dance). Yesterday I . . . . (danced)."

EXERCISE 44

PRESENT	PAST
1. wash	
2. fill	
3. twist	
4. dress	
5. choke	
6. mend	
7. rain	
8. land	
9. mail	
10. test	

Verbs of being change in form to agree with the subject. The five verbs of being are:

1. _____
2. _____
3. _____
4. _____
5. _____

EXERCISE 45

Write the correct form of the present and past tense of the verbs of being for the subjects below.

PRESENT		PAST
1. I	7. He	
2. She	8. I	
3. You	9. We	
4. We	10. She	
5. They	11. You	
6. It	12. They	

EXERCISE 46

Verbs that have a different form in the past tense are called *irregular* verbs. Write the past tense for each verb below.

PRESENT	PAST
1. dig	
2. run	
3. sing	
4. think	
5. fly	
6. sit	
7. drink	
8. win	
9. bring	
10. sink	

Can you think of more irregular verbs? Write them in the spaces below. (See Exercises 34 and 35.)

11.	
12.	
13.	

14. _____   _____

EXERCISE 47

What is wrong with the following sentences? Can you correct them?

Example
  I started the car and drive down the street.
  (Corrected)
  I started the car and drove down the street.

  Use the first verb in the sentence to determine the tense of the second verb.

1. First we eat breakfast and then we went to school.

2. Mary cut Anne's hair and curls it.

3. The mother fed and changes the baby.

4. You wash the dishes and I dried them.

5. We ate and drink well.

6. The boys fight and yelled at each other.

7. The policeman stops his car and walked over to the boys.

8. The fire engine roared down the street and skids around the corner.

9. I went to the movies and then I come home.

10. I am in a hurry but he was not.

Review Test of Verbs

EXERCISE 48

A. Diagram the following sentences.

  1. The three boys fished all day in the river.

2. Bass, pickerel, and trout were their catch.

3. Low in the sky sank the sun.

4. The evening shadows crept across the valley.

5. Home went the boys with their catch.

6. Their supper that night was delicious fresh fish.

7. Tim, Jack, and Joe were old friends.

8. They often went fishing together.

9. One day they saw a school of pickerel.

10. Now they watch the river every day.

B. In the sentences above, find examples of the following.

  1. A proper noun_____

  2. A common singular noun_____

  3. A collective noun_____

  4. A verb of being_____

  5. A verb of action in the past tense_____

  6. A direct object_____

  7. A compound subject_____

  8. A pronoun_____

  9. A verb in the present tense_____

  10. A predicate noun_____

C. Write the singular or the plural of each of the following nouns.

SINGULAR	PLURAL
1. woman	_____
2. lady	_____

3. boy _____

4. wish _____

5. gentleman _____

6. _____ mice

7. _____ houses

8. _____ geese

9. _____ days

10. _____ knives

D. Write the past or present tense of each verb below.

PRESENT	PAST
1. wash	_____
2. go	_____
3. fly	_____
4. sing	_____
5. think	_____
6. am	_____
7. want	_____
8. creep	_____
9. watch	_____
10. run	_____
11. _____	wandered
12. _____	rang
13. _____	bought

14. _____ were

15. _____ swam

16. _____ stopped

17. _____ was

18. _____ belonged

19. _____ wore

20. _____ blossomed

E. Put a suitable pronoun before each of these verbs of being.

1. _____ am

2. _____ was

3. _____ were

4. _____ are

5. _____ is

F. Put a suitable verb of being in each of the following spaces.

1. Yesterday he _____ here.

2. Tomorrow I _____ going home.

3. They _____ at the picnic last week.

4. She _____ the happiest person I know.

5. We _____ leaving right now.

Give yourself 5 points for each sentence correctly diagramed. Take 2 points off for each error. Give yourself 1 point for each item on the rest of the test. Did you get at least 80? If not, go back and review your mistakes.

Chapter 5

Four Kinds of Sentences

So far we have been talking about the most common type of sentence: *a statement* of some kind. A sentence that makes a statement always ends with a period.

Example

This is Monday, June 5.

There are also other kinds of sentences. *Questions* are easy to spot. They usually begin with the verb and always end with a question mark.

Example

Is this Monday?

Exclamations express excitement or emotion of some kind and end with an exclamation mark.

Example

What a terrible thing to do!

The fourth and last kind of sentence is the *command*. It may begin with "please," but it is still a request or an order. The subject (you) is usually implied rather than stated.

Examples

(You) Stand up straight.
Please (you) pass the salt.

These periods, exclamation marks, and question marks are called *punctuation*. The same sentence with different punctuation expresses different meanings.

Examples

Joe hit Jim.   *Statement*
(Did) Joe hit Jim?   *Question*
Joe, hit Jim.   *Command*
Joe hit Jim!   *Exclamation*

Marie has done her work.   *Statement*
Marie, have you done your work?   *Question*
Marie, (you) do your work.   *Command*
Marie did her work!   *Exclamation*

Statements and Questions

EXERCISE 49

A sentence is a group of words expressing a complete thought. A sentence which makes a statement begins with a capital and is followed by a period.

45

Example

The janitor went to the door.

A sentence which asks a question begins with a capital and is followed by a question mark.

Example

Where did the janitor go?

Read each of the following sentences and after it write *S* if it is a statement and *Q* if it is a question. Put a period or question mark after each sentence.

1. What do you want_____

2. I want to go with you_____

3. Jim hit John_____

4. Why did he do that_____

5. It was not John's fault_____

6. Jim has a nasty temper_____

7. Where are you going_____

8. I am going to work_____

9. Do you like your boss_____

10. No, he is too crabby_____

How many questions did you find?_____

EXERCISE 50

Read each of the following sentences and after it write *S* if it is a statement and *Q* if it is a question. Put a period or question mark after each sentence.

1. What shall we do now_____

2. Shall we go fishing_____

3. No, I don't feel like fishing_____

4. Would you like some ice cream_____

5. This is good, isn't it_____

6. Tomorrow is my day off_____

7. What will you do_____

8. I hope it doesn't rain_____

9. I have to paint the house_____

10. Wouldn't you like to help me_____

Commands and Exclamations

EXERCISE 51

Besides *statements* and *questions* there are two more kinds of sentences.

1. A *command* begins with a capital and ends with a period, like a statement.
    The subject is always *you*, but it is often left out.

    (You) Keep off the grass.
    (You) Pass the butter, please.

2. A sentence that expresses excitement or strong feeling is called an *exclamation*. It begins with a capital and ends with an exclamation mark.

    Something terrible has happened!
    Hurry! We need the doctor!

After each of the following sentences write *C* for command or *E* for exclamation.

1. Go on home now._____

2. Oh! I forgot something!_____

3. Turn off the headlights. _____

4. Quick! Call the police!_____

5. Please shut the door._____

6. Don't walk on the grass._____

7. Hey! Guess what happened! _____

8. Call me up tonight. _____

9. Long live the king! _____

10. Please pass in your papers. _____

EXERCISE 52

After each of the following sentences write C for command or E for exclamation. Add (you) before the verb in each command.

1. Hand me that book. _____

2. Hear this. Now hear this. _____

3. What a wonderful idea! _____

4. Gee, that would be great! _____

5. Please tell me what happened. _____

6. It's a deep, dark secret! _____

7. Turn right at the corner. _____

8. Holy cow, look at that! _____

9. Get a move on, you guys. _____

10. Get going before you get caught. _____

Identifying Sentences

EXERCISE 53

The four kinds of sentences begin with capitals and end with periods, question marks, or exclamation marks.

Question ?
Statement .
Command (You) .
Exclamation !

Tell what kind of sentence each of the following is by writing the correct letter after it: Q for question, S for statement, C for command, and E for exclamation.

1. What time is it? _____

2. Drop that gun. _____

3. George was late to work. _____

4. Nina, come here at once. _____

5. Don't you think Patty reads well? _____

6. The telephone rang for a long time. _____

7. How fast the children ran! _____

8. Please put it on the table. _____

9. May I borrow that book? _____

10. Joe needs another pencil. _____

EXERCISE 54

Tell what kind of sentence each of the following is by writing the correct letter after it: Q for question, S for statement, C for command, and E for exclamation.

1. Come in, please. _____

2. Why are you late? _____

3. Quick, call a doctor. _____

4. That is a pretty dress. _____

5. Do you like it? _____

6. I think it's lovely! _____

7. It is time for lunch. _____

8. Do you like to swim? _____

9. Close that window. _____

10. It's a beautiful day._____

Review Test of Sentences

EXERCISE 55

A. Write the correct word in the blank.

1. What kind of sentence ends with a question mark?_____

2. What kind of sentence makes a statement of fact?_____

3. What kind of sentence has an implied subject *You*?_____

4. What kind of sentence expresses excitement?_____

5. What must every sentence begin with?

_____

B. Put in capitals and punctuation and tell what kind of sentence each of the following is.

1. please pass the butter_____

2. why are you so late_____

3. it is much colder tonight_____

4. my goodness, what a surprise _____

5. what happened_____

6. somebody got hurt_____

7. gosh, that's terrible_____

8. did you call a doctor_____

9. help, call the police_____

10. they're already here_____

C. Punctuate and tell what kind of sentence each of the following is.

1. what time is it_____

2. it is seven o'clock_____

3. pass the bread, please_____

4. it is time for bed_____

5. get to bed, boys _____

6. Henry broke his leg_____

7. how did he do that_____

8. quick, get a doctor_____

9. get Dr. Fox on the telephone_____

10. he's coming right over_____

11. what are you doing_____

12. it's none of your business_____

13. don't get fresh with me_____

14. are you looking for trouble_____

15. gosh, you must be nuts_____

16. why don't you get lost_____

17. I have a sore throat_____

18. get out of the way _____

19. do you think you can win _____

20. ouch, that hurt_____

Give yourself 2 points for each sentence in A and 3 points for those in B and C. Take off 1 point for each mistake. Did you get at least 80? Do you understand your errors?

Chapter 6

Complete and Incomplete Sentences

We have now learned a good deal about sentences. We have seen that every sentence

1. Is made up of a subject and a predicate.
2. Contains a noun or pronoun which is the main word in the subject.
3. Contains a verb of action or being which is the main word in the predicate.
4. Begins with a capital letter and ends with a period, question mark, or exclamation mark.

We have also studied the structure of sentences through diagraming, and we know that verbs of action are often followed by objects which receive that action.

Example

> The batter hit the ball.

Verbs of being, on the other hand, are followed by predicate nouns which are simply a way of describing the subject.

Examples

> I am an engineer.
> My brother is a Democrat.

We know also that there are different kinds of sentences (statements, commands, questions, and exclamations) but that all correct sentences must express a complete thought. Many beginners have difficulty with this. They have not learned that sentences must have a subject and a predicate and express one complete thought. Frequently, several complete thoughts are strung together in what are called *run-on sentences*.

Example

> Jerry and I went to the drugstore for
> a soda we stayed there all afternoon.

This should be two separate sentences since it expresses two different complete thoughts.

> Jerry and I went to the drugstore for a soda.
> We stayed there all afternoon.

Another common error is the *incomplete sentence*, which does not have a subject or a predicate, or is unfinished in meaning.

Example

> When we went out to lunch.

The reader never knows what happened at lunch. In order to avoid such errors, remember always to ask yourself:
"What is the action taking place?"
"Who or what performs that action?"
If your sentence contains these basic requirements, it expresses a complete thought.

49

Complete Sentences

EXERCISE 56

A sentence expresses a complete thought. It begins with a captial and ends with a period. If the sentence asks a question, it ends with a question mark instead of a period. If it expresses excitement, it is followed by an exclamation mark instead of a period. These marks are called *punctuation*.

Read the following groups of words and draw a line through each one that is not a complete thought.

Put a capital letter at the beginning and the proper punctuation at the end of each one which is a complete sentence.

Example A walked into the house
This is not a complete sentence because it does not tell you *who* walked in. Therefore a line should be drawn through it.

Example B the boys walked into the house
This expresses a complete thought so it should begin with a capital and end with a period.

The boys walked into the house.

1. went down the street

2. two girls went down the street

3. they waited on the corner

4. running down the path

5. when she went in the house

6. suddenly a voice

7. suddenly Nancy heard a voice

8. in the gray light of dawn

9. the boys went fishing

10. and ran to the window

How many complete sentences did you find?_____

EXERCISE 57

Read the following groups of words and draw a line through each one that is not a complete thought. Put a capital letter at the beginning and the proper punctuation at the end of each one which is a complete sentence.

1. three cars are

2. three cars are colliding

3. the cop on the corner

4. the cop on the corner has a gun

5. after my lunch

6. soon the bell rang

7. turned on the light

8. my mother turned on the light

9. when the doorbell rang

10. when the doorbell rang I opened the door

Incomplete Sentences

EXERCISE 58

The following are *not* complete sentences. On the line under each group of words, write a sentence using these words to express a complete thought.

1. when the siren sounded

_____

_____

2. rushing downstairs, Sally

_____

_____

3. Norman said that he

_____

_____

4. and sat down to watch TV

_____

_____

5. on a hot summer day

_____

_____

6. like to swim

_____

_____

7. John and Bill also

_____

_____

8. rang again and again

_____

_____

9. up the ladder

_____

_____

10. later in the day

_____

_____

Did you remember the capitals at the beginning?

3. my lunch at work

_____

_____

4. I wish I had taken

_____

_____

5. too cold to go

_____

_____

6. right after breakfast

_____

_____

7. standing quietly in the corner

_____

_____

8. their friends and relatives

_____

_____

9. before dark

_____

_____

10. it was very

_____

_____

EXERCISE 59

The following are *not* complete sentences. On the line under each group of words, write a sentence using these words to express a complete thought.

1. ran into the house

_____

_____

2. the lamp on the table

_____

_____

Run-on Sentences

EXERCISE 60

A sentence is a group of words which expresses only one complete thought. Different thoughts should be separated from each other in different sentences, not strung together in one. This common mistake is called a *run-on sentence*.

In the examples below, make each run-on sentence into two or three separate sentences, each one containing a complete thought, by using capitals and punctuation correctly.

Example

Tom came home he had supper his brother and he went out to play ball

This should be:

Tom came home. He had supper. His brother and he went out to play ball.

1. your letter came yesterday I read it afterwards I showed it to my buddy

2. his umbrella blew away in the wind it went flying down the street

3. the cat was angry she started clawing me then I hit her

4. my wife asked me to go to the store I forgot all about it

5. someone called my name I turned around there was my friend Joe

6. I read about him in the paper it said he was a great pitcher

7. Jim wanted to go to the movies his girl friend wanted to go dancing

8. a big plane was flying over the house suddenly we heard an explosion we ran outside

9. all we could see was dust then suddenly flames sprang up

10. people were screaming I tried to get close the flames were too hot

There are 25 complete thoughts in the sentences above. Did you find them all? Count your sentences.

EXERCISE 61

Follow the same directions as for Exercise 60.

1. after the show we went to the drugstore we each had a Coke

2. yesterday was my mother's birthday I forgot to buy her a present

3. he heard a noise it was outside his window

4. when she left work it was raining she took a taxi home

5. it's too cold in here I think I'll get my sweater

6. my brother asked me to drive him to work I couldn't because my car was being repaired

7. last night we came home late we got caught in a traffic jam

8. I wish I had a bike then I could ride to work

9. she starts her new job this week I hope she likes it

10. maybe they will visit us soon we enjoy their company

How many sentences did you find?_____

Review Test of Sentences

EXERCISE 62

A. 1. What is a sentence?

_____

2. What are the two parts of a sentence?

_____

3. What must a sentence begin with?

_____

4. What must a sentence end with?

_____

5. What is a run-on sentence?

_____

B. The following include complete sentences, incomplete sentences, and run-on sentences.
   a.) Punctuate the complete sentences.
   b.) Draw a line through the incomplete sentences.
   c.) Separate the run-on sentences and punctuate properly.

1. where are you going, my pretty maid

2. after we go to the show

3. I would like a drink of water

4. he went to work then he came home for dinner

5. because it is so hot

6. first she wrote the report after that she went to the meeting

7. after all that, she was tired out

8. he's a big tall guy with red hair

9. although he gets his work done

10. first he did setting-up exercises then he took a hot shower

C. Make sentences using these groups of words and write them on the lines below. Be sure to use capitals, question marks, or exclamation marks where needed.

1. my father and I

_____

2. where did you

_____

3. the planet Mars

_____

4. oh, my goodness

_____

5. ran faster than ever

_____

6. why were they

_____

7. the people in our car pool

_____
_____

8. out of the window

_____
_____

9. fell flat on his face

_____
_____

10. the teacher's dress

_____
_____

11. when did she

_____
_____

12. the fellows in this block

_____
_____

13. ran down the street

_____
_____

14. with the siren screaming

_____
_____

15. good heavens

_____
_____

16. what is that

_____
_____

17. the last thing

_____
_____

18. did he ask

_____
_____

19. out the window

_____
_____

20. why in the world

_____
_____

Give yourself 3 points for each sentence in **B** and **C**, 2 points each for **A**. Check your own capitals and punctuation in **C**.

Chapter 7

Punctuation

Correct punctuation is very important in writing. Punctuation can change the whole meaning of a sentence.

Examples

Don hit him.
Don, hit him!

A comma, as in the sentence above, indicates a pause, and is used to separate or set off the name of the person spoken to. That sentence is really a command, with *you* as the implied subject.

Example

Don, (you) hit him!

Commas are also used to separate quotations of what people say from the rest of the sentence.

Example

Jim said, "Let's go swimming."
or
"Let's go swimming," said Jim.

Note that if the quotation precedes the rest of the sentence, it ends with a comma rather than a period because the sentence is not complete. Quotation marks turn in toward the words which are being quoted: " before the beginning and " after the comma or period which ends the quotation.

Quotations

There are three things to remember about quotations.
1. Whenever a person's words are repeated exactly they must be set off from the rest of the sentence by quotation marks *before* and *after* them.
2. The quotation must begin with a capital, and it must end with a period if it ends the sentence.
3. The quotation must be separated from the rest of the sentence by a comma.

EXERCISE 63

Place commas, periods, and quotation marks in the right places.

Example
    Marie said, "My kitten is black and white."

1. The supervisor said Let's start our meeting

2. Alex announced Our new cleaning products are very popular

3. Mary stated We made a large profit from them in the first six months

4. Susan remarked They sell best in the Middle West

5. Bill replied That's where we have done the most advertising

6. Mary suggested We need more radio ads in

other parts of the country

7. Alex said It's important to find out why our customers prefer our products

8. Susan said Let's make a survey of our customers in the Middle West

9. Bill answered That's a great idea

10. The supervisor said Now we'll discuss those radio ads

EXERCISE 64

In the following sentences put in punctuation (commas, periods, and quotation marks) and change lower case letters to capitals where needed.

1. Sarah announced I'd like to go camping for our vacation

2. Bob said that's impossible because we don't have any camping equipment

3. Sarah answered we could borrow the Nelsons' equipment

4. Bob said OK, but we need to decide where we're going

5. Sarah suggested I think Ontario would be a lovely place to camp

6. Bob sighed yes, but that would be a long drive

7. Sarah replied well, we could camp along the way

8. Bob said but we have only two weeks of vacation

9. Sarah said I guess that isn't enough time

10. Bob suggested we could camp at one of the state parks near here

EXERCISE 65

Sometimes the quotation comes first in a sen-

tence. In that case, instead of a period at the end of the quotation, a comma is used to separate it from the rest of the sentence.

Example

"I love football," said Bernie.

Put commas, quotation marks, and periods in the right places.

1. I got a raise announced Sally at dinner

2. I'm very pleased to hear it exclaimed her mother

3. You've worked very hard for that said her father

4. I think this calls for a celebration he added

5. I think so, too Sally's mother said

6. I don't see anything so great about it growled her brother

7. That's just because you're jealous snapped back Sally

8. Now don't quarrel at dinner said their mother

9. I was going to suggest a treat for all of us their father remarked

10. In that case, it's OK with me announced Sally's brother

EXERCISE 66

Put in punctuation and capitals as above. In this exercise, the quotation may come before or after the rest of the sentence. See how much more interesting the story sounds than it did in Exercise 64.

1. I'd like to go camping for our vacation Sarah announced

2. Bob said that's impossible because we don't have any camping equipment

3. We could borrow the Nelsons' equipment Sarah answered

4. Bob said OK, but we need to decide where we're going

5. Sarah suggested I think Ontario would be a lovely place to camp

6. Yes, but that would be a long drive Bob sighed

7. Sarah replied well, we could camp along the way

8. But we have only two weeks of vacation Bob said

9. Sarah said I guess that isn't enough time

10. We could camp at one of the state parks near here Bob suggested

Questions and Exclamations in Quotations

Like ordinary sentences, quotations may end in question marks or exclamation marks instead of periods. If such a quotation comes at the beginning of a sentence, it does *not* need a comma to separate it from the rest of the sentence. The question mark or exclamation mark is enough punctuation.

Examples
"Hello!" called the cheerful lady.
"How are you today?" she said, smiling.

EXERCISE 67

Punctuate the following and insert quotation marks in the right places.

1. Where are you going asked the young woman

2. I'm going running answered the young man

3. Can I come with you she asked

4. Of course you can he exclaimed

5. I like having company when I run he added

6. Oh, and I love the exercise said the young woman

7. When did you start running asked the young man

8. I started about two years ago she said

9. I wanted to keep in shape she added

10. Come on, let's go he said

EXERCISE 68

Sometimes a person says more than one thing at a time. You may have a quotation of two or more sentences, with the reference to the person who is speaking coming between the quotations.

Example
"Turn off that radio," said my father. "I can't hear myself think!"

Punctuate the following sentences.

1. Where am I asked the bearded man

2. You are in the hospital said the nurse

3. The hospital Good heavens exclaimed the man

4. Now, don't get excited the nurse said We will take good care of you

5. What happened to me asked the man

6. You were hit by a car said the nurse Don't you remember anything

7. I remember riding my motorcycle the man

said I don't know what happened after that

8. Am I going to get well he asked

9. Of course you are exclaimed the nurse The

doctor will soon be here

10. Thank goodness for that sighed the man

Review Test of Punctuation

EXERCISE 69

Every sentence begins with a capital and ends with a period. Questions end with a question mark, and exclamations end with an exclamation mark.

A. Put quotation marks around each of the following sentences and capitals and punctuation marks in the proper place. On the following line, name the kind of sentence by its first letter: S, Q, C, or E.

1. where on earth have you been _____

2. heavens, you had me worried to death _____

3. don't you ever run off like that again _____

4. I was afraid you had been run over _____

5. why didn't you telephone me _____

6. I would have come and picked you up _____

7. listen to me when I'm talking to you _____

8. you are simply impossible _____

9. you owe me an explanation _____

10. good gracious, she's running away again _____

B. Put capitals, punctuation, and quotation marks in the right places in the following sentences.

1. where are you going asked the police officer

2. I'm not telling the little boy said

3. the police officer looked at him and asked

what's your name

4. I won't tell you answered the boy

5. does your mother know you're out asked

the officer

6. the little boy muttered no

7. don't you think she'll worry the officer said

8. she won't care said the little boy

9. here comes a lady now said the officer

10. Billy, where have you been the lady cried

you had me worried sick

Give yourself 5 points for each correct sentence. Take off 2 points for each mistake. Correct your mistakes before you go on.

Chapter 8

Capital Letters

We have already discussed the major uses of capital letters: for the first word in a sentence, and for proper nouns which are the names of persons, places, or specific things, such as the *Empire State Building*. It is sometimes difficult to decide when a capital should be used. For example, *my mother,* as one of many mothers, would not be capitalized; but *Mother,* used as a name for a specific person, would be.

Example
>Our family's church is The
>First Baptist Church.

Here the first *church* is not capitalized because it refers to churches in general. *The First Baptist Church* is the title of a specific church; it is, therefore, capitalized.

There are other uses for capitals, chiefly in poetry and religious prose. Modern practices, however, are changing. Traditionally, every line of a poem or a hymn begins with a capital letter. Religious references to God, the Lord, the Virgin Mother, and the Holy Spirit are also capitalized. The pronouns *Thee* and *Thou* which refer to God always used to be capitalized, but that practice is changing with the modern usage of *you* and *your*.

Capitals are used for exclamations such as *Oh,* for the pronoun *I,* and for all important words in a title, including the first. They are also used for initials and for titles such as *Reverend,* which, although it may be abbreviated to *Rev.,* still retains a capital.

The following exercises will give practice in all these uses of capital letters.

Rules for Capitals

A capital is used

1. for the first word in a sentence.

2. for the first word in a line of poetry.

3. for days of the week, months, and holidays.

4. for the name of a particular person, place, or thing—in other words, a proper noun.

EXERCISE 70

Put a capital above the proper letter wherever it is needed in these sentences.

1. this is the first day of october.

2. tom and dick both live in springfield.

3. star light, star bright,

   first star I see tonight.

4. marie and ellen live in pittsburgh.

5. thank you for the book you sent me for

   christmas.

6. should old acquaintance be forgot and

    never brought to mind?

    should old acquaintance be forgot and

    days of auld lang syne?

7. columbus discovered america on october

    12, 1492.

8. rick brought katie to the party.

9. there is a zoo in central park in the middle of

    new york city.

10. george washington lived in mt. vernon,

    virginia.

EXERCISE 71

Put in capitals and punctuation marks in the following sentences.

1. my birthday is on saturday, october 23

2. joe's birthday is the next day, sunday

3. joe and victor are my best friends

4. the president of the united states lives in the

    white house

5. roses are red, violets are blue,

    sugar is sweet and so are you

6. i love christmas even better than thanksgiving

7. columbia university is in new york city

8. dr. fisher is our family doctor

9. near us is the coliseum

10. my country, 'tis of thee,

    sweet land of liberty,

    of thee I sing

More Rules for Capitals

1. Capitals are used for *I* and *O* or *Oh*.

Example
>   Oh dear, I am late for work!

2. Capitals are used for words referring to God.

Example
>   Hear me, O Lord, when I cry unto Thee;
>   I will sing praises unto my God.

3. Capitals are used for the first word and for all important words in a title. Titles of books and other publications are underlined.

Example
>   Our English book is called Step-by-Step
>   Guide to Correct English.

EXERCISE 72

Put capitals where needed in the following sentences.

1. o give thanks unto the lord for he is good.

2. i wish i had a new ford.

3. my father reads the daily news.

4. oh nuts, i forgot my lunch!

5. why, o why, am i so stupid?

6. the wind in the willows is a good book.

7. show me thy ways, o lord; teach me thy paths.

8. have you read the adventures of tom sawyer?

9. my composition is called the first president of the united states.

10. the lord is my shepherd; i shall not want.

Put capitals where needed in the following poem.

THE DAFFODILS

i wandered lonely as a cloud
that floats on high o'er vales and hills,
when all at once i saw a crowd,
a host of golden daffodils,
beside the lake, beneath the trees,
fluttering and dancing in the breeze.

William Wordsworth

Initials and Abbreviations

Every initial is written with a capital and is followed by a period.

Example

James Frick Sawyer—J. F. Sawyer

Most abbreviations begin with capitals and end with periods.

Example

Captain Joshua Booth—Capt. J. Booth
Doctor Daniel Berman—Dr. D. Berman

EXERCISE 73

Put capitals and periods where needed in the following sentences.

1. my name is joseph w wiley

2. i live at 3 rutland rd in great neck, n y

3. the ship is commanded by capt peter smith

4. the director of the f b i lives in washington, d c

5. gen johnson commands the armed forces of the u s a

6. i got a b s degree from city college

7. rev keating lives at 35 w fourteenth st, n y c

8. mr and mrs j williams, jr live at 19 lynn rd, springdale, mass

9. samuel schulman, m d has an office in the medical bldg

10. his office hours begin at 10 a m

EXERCISE 74

What do these initials stand for? Look in the dictionary for those you do not know.

1. P. M. _____

2. F. B. I. _____

3. B. C. _____

4. A. D. _____

5. U. N. _____

6. P. O. _____

7. U. S. A. _____

8. N. Y. C. _____

9. M. D. _____

10. A. M. _____

Practice in Capitals and Abbreviations

EXERCISE 75

Put capitals and periods where needed in these sentences.

1. thomas jefferson wrote the declaration of independence

2. george washington was our first president

3. abraham lincoln composed the gettysburg address

4. the battle of bunker hill began the american revolution

5. the liberty bell is in a museum in philadelphia

6. the empire state building used to be the tallest building in the world

7. radio city is at 49th st and fifth ave in new york

8. the mississippi river flows into the gulf of mexico

9. hawaii and alaska are our newest states

10. children believe santa claus lives at the north pole

EXERCISE 76

Write the abbreviations for

1. Street _____

2. Road _____

3. January _____

4. December _____

5. Monday _____

6. Tuesday _____

7. Wednesday _____

8. October _____

9. Nebraska _____

10. Connecticut _____

11. Thursday _____

12. February _____

13. Massachusetts _____

14. Friday _____

15. November _____

16. Mountain _____

17. Doctor _____

18. Professor _____

19. Saturday _____

20. General _____

Review of Capitals

Capitals are used for

1. the first word in a sentence.

2. the first word in a line of poetry.

3. days of the week, months, and holidays.

4. the name of a particular person, place, or thing.

5. *I* and *O* or *Oh.*

6. words referring to God.

7. initials.

8. the important words in titles.

9. most abbreviations.

Review Test of Capitals

EXERCISE 77

A. Put capitals and periods wherever needed in the following sentences.

1. george, elvis, and john have a rock group, the weirdos

2. thanksgiving day comes on november 22 this year

3. dr anderson lives in mt hermon, mass

4. hear me, oh lord, when i pray unto thee

5. julie's father is in the f b i

6. prof dennis teaches at columbia university

7. the name of my book is a tale of two cities

8. saturday is my favorite day of the week

9. i will send your package c o d to 231 main st, springfield, mass

10. sing a song of seasons,

    something bright in all,

    flowers in the summer,

    fires in the fall!

B. Punctuate the following sentences. Put capitals where needed.

1. where are you going asked my brother

2. out to play baseball i answered

3. he shouted after me hey, can i come

4. oh i guess so i said

5. we headed down main street toward prospect park

6. dr j f robbins works at the dallas city hospital

7. corp g steward lives at 10 main st denver col

8. judy said she would be home by 12 p m

9. she didn't come until 2 a m

10. boys flying kites haul in their white-winged birds

    you can't do that way when you're flying words

    thoughts unexpressed may sometimes fall back dead

    but god himself can't change them once they're said

                                    Will Carlton

Give yourself 5 points for each correct sentence. Take off 1 point for each mistake. Be sure you understand why you made errors.

Chapter 9

Adjectives

Adjectives are words that *describe* nouns or pronouns. These are the words that give life and color and fill out the bare bones of a sentence. Notice the difference that adjectives make in the two sentences below.

Examples

The guard approached the prisoner.
The huge, powerful, angry guard approached the frightened, cowering prisoner.

The words *huge*, *powerful*, and *angry* all describe the guard menacingly approaching the *frightened*, *cowering* prisoner.

Adjectives are usually found just before the noun that they *describe* or *modify*, although sometimes they follow it as in this sentence:

Example

The prisoner, frightened and cowering, shrank into the corner of his cell.

Often adjectives follow a verb of being; and, although they are then part of the predicate, they describe the subject. These are called *predicate adjectives*.

Examples

I am hungry.
Her dress was elegant.

Most adjectives have three forms which are used in comparing qualities.

Example

Jim is tall. (*Tall* describes Jim, even though it is in the predicate.)

Joe is taller than Jim. (There must be two of anything in order to compare them.)

Harry is the tallest. (There must be three or more to compare before this form can be used.)

Most adjectives can be compared simply by adding *er* or *est*. The rest can be compared by adding the words *more* or *most* in front of them.

Example

Sally is beautiful.
Nina is more beautiful.
But Joanna is the most beautiful girl I know.

There are also a few irregular adjectives which change in form as they are compared. Some examples are *good*, *better*, and *best*. These you will have to memorize.

Some adjectives cannot be compared because they are already "the most." Words like *perfect* or *empty* cannot be compared. If a thing is perfect, how can it be more perfect? *Unique* is another such word. If there is only one such thing in the world, then there is nothing to be compared with it.

63

Last of all, there are a number of little words which do not seem to describe very much but, in fact, act as adjectives. These are words such as *each*, *which*, *my*, *some*, and *what*. Along with them we will group *the*, *a*, and *an*, the words called articles. As we have already seen (p.19), they refer to specific or nonspecific nouns. All of these words add meaning and clarity to the sentence in which they are used.

Descriptive Adjectives

EXERCISE 78

An *adjective* is a word that describes a noun, giving it color and meaning. It is usually found just before the noun it *describes* or *modifies*.

Diagram these sentences and circle the descriptive adjectives. There are at least thirty adjectives. Can you find them?

Example
The fat red hen / waddled across the dusty yard.

1. The slim, long-haired girl waited on a busy corner.

2. She wore a pink shirt and ragged blue jeans.

3. My new car has bucket seats and red upholstery.

4. The big brown dog chased the frightened thief.

5. The brightest girl on our block is little Beth.

6. The big black cat sat in the sunny window of the grocery store.

7. On cold winter nights I like a blazing fire.

8. The icy wind blows stinging snow down the narrow streets.

9. But in our cheerful kitchen is a warm stove.

10. His plump rosy mother hums an old Italian song while she cooks delicious lasagna.

EXERCISE 79

Fill the spaces below with adjectives to describe the nouns in the sentences.

1. The_____girls giggled as the_____ boys walked by.

2. A_____skyscraper is being built overlooking the _____bay.

3. A_____breeze blew in from the_____ ocean.

4. He drove his_____convertible down the_____highway.

5. A_____basket of flowers stood on the _____table.

6. A_____girl rode on the_____ bicycle.

7. The_____boy was eating_____ ice cream with_____sauce.

8. In my grandmother's_____house I could smell a_____pie baking.

9. On Monday morning the woman wore a _____blouse and a_____skirt.

10. She had _____shoes and a_____ pocketbook.

Predicate Adjectives

EXERCISE 80

An adjective often precedes the noun it modifies. But sometimes an adjective is found in the predicate after a verb of being. It is called a *predicate adjective* if it modifies the subject, which may be a noun or a pronoun.

Examples
I / am happy.   The barn / is red.

In these examples *happy* describes how I am, and the adjective *red* describes the barn just as much as if the phrase "the red barn" had been used instead.

Diagram the following sentences and draw an arrow to connect the predicate adjective with the subject it modifies.

1. My house is green.

2. The supper was delicious.

3. The boys were noisy.

4. Your picture is beautiful.

5. The weather was hot.

6. But the evenings were cool.

7. I am busy this week.

8. That school is big.

9. My boss is strict.

10. But she is fair.

EXERCISE 81

In the following sentences both ordinary adjectives and predicate adjectives will be found. Diagram the sentences and connect each adjective with an arrow to the noun or pronoun it modifies.

1. My house is white with green shutters.

2. My rattly old car was blue.

3. His new convertible is red with a black top.

4. The cool cotton dress is blue and white.

5. The young people were happy and noisy.

6. I am sad and lonely tonight.

7. We are crowded in our small apartment.

8. The park is lovely in the warm spring weather.

9. The busy highway is full of speeding cars.

10. The giant plane is high over the gray storm clouds.

Comparing Adjectives

EXERCISE 82

An *adjective* is a word that describes a noun or a pronoun. When you wish to compare two nouns, you change the form of the adjective, usually by adding *er*.

Examples
John is tall.
Ricky is taller than John.
Which apple is smaller (of the two apples)?

If you are comparing three or more nouns, add *est* to the adjective.

Examples
Judy is the brightest student in the class.
Tom is the shortest boy on the team.

After each of the following sentences, state how many nouns are being compared: two, or three, or more.

Examples

My car is faster than yours. (Compares two cars. Write 2.)

I have the strictest teacher in the school. (Compares three or more teachers. Write 3+.)

1. I am taller than my brother. _____

2. My father is the tallest in the family. _____

3. You are the nicest person I know. _____

4. My brother is much older than I. _____

5. She has the cutest baby I ever saw! _____

6. Selma and Judy are both pretty but Judy is prettier than Selma. _____

7. A quarter is larger than a dime. _____

8. Tokyo is the largest city in the world. _____

9. My sister is the best lawyer in town. _____

10. The World Trade Center is higher than the Empire State Building. _____

EXERCISE 83

Compare the adjectives listed below by adding *er* or *est*. If the adjective already ends in e, add *r* or *st*. If the adjective ends in *y*, change the *y* to *i* before adding *er* or *est*.

Example

ADJECTIVE	MORE	MOST
small	smaller	smallest

1. great _____ _____

2. gentle _____ _____

3. high _____ _____

4. lovely _____ _____

5. smart _____ _____

6. funny _____ _____

7. blue _____ _____

8. pale _____ _____

9. tiny _____ _____

10. tame _____ _____

Irregular Adjectives

There are a number of words which do not seem to describe very much but act, in fact, as adjectives. Typical of these are *my, his, your, some, few, these, that,* and *hers.*

Examples

Some time	Which hat	Few people
That boy	These days	My mother
Each year	Many months	Every week

EXERCISE 84

The words *the, a,* and *an* act as adjectives, too. The word *the* refers to a specific noun. "Put *the* book on *the* table," refers to a specific book and a specific table. "Get me *a* book," refers to any book, not a particular one.

The word *a* is used before words beginning with *consonants* (hard sounds, such as *b, d, t, k*). The word *an* is used before words beginning with *vowels* (*a, e, i, o, u,*) because it sounds better to have vowel sounds separated by the consonant *n*, as in "an egg" or "an umbrella." *An* is also used before words beginning with a silent *h*, as in *honest.*

Examples

A man   An honest man

Before each of the nouns below, write *a* or *an*, depending upon whether the following word begins with a vowel, a consonant, or a silent *h*.

1. _____ tree

2. _____ apple

3. _____ table

4. _____ ocean

5. _____ elevator

6. _____ pencil

7. _____ automobile

8. _____ honor

9. _____ lamp

10. _____ Indian

Some adjectives are irregular and use different words to express *more* or *the most* instead of adding *er* and *est*. Here are a few of the most common ones which should be memorized.

ADJECTIVE	MORE	MOST
good, well	better	best
bad	worse	worst
little	less	least
much, many	more	most
far	further	furthest

EXERCISE 85

In the following sentences, draw arrows from all adjectives, including *the* and *a* or *an*, to the nouns or pronouns they modify.

Example
The old farmer was tired.

1. The apples from his farm are best.

2. She wore a little red bow in her blond hair.

3. I hope you are better today.

4. You are a bad dancer but your sister is worse.

5. The ice cream vendor pushed his little cart.

6. We had delicious beef, fried potatoes, and green beans.

7. It is a good thing you have an old uncle with that much energy.

8. The TV in the next apartment makes a terrible noise.

9. I want an honest answer to my last question.

10. An eagle is faster than most birds.

Review Test of Adjectives

EXERCISE 86

A. Fill in the following blanks.

1. An adjective describes a _____ or a _____.

2. A predicate adjective modifies or describes the _____ of the sentence.

3. *A* is an indefinite adjective used before words beginning with a _____.

4. *An* is an indefinite adjective used before words beginning with a _____.

B. Diagram the following sentences. Draw arrows from each adjective to the noun or pronoun it describes.

1. The big black dog followed the tall man.

2. A white fluffy kitten sat on the front stoop.

3. My old grandmother is deaf.

4. But she is a marvelous cook.

5. In the pouring rain he ran home.

6. He had forgotten an umbrella.

7. My younger son is now taller than I am!.

8. Few people are smarter than you are.

9. That boy is the fastest runner on the track

team.

10. My wife knows which desserts I like.

C. Compare the following:

ADJECTIVE	MORE	MOST
1. funny	_____	_____
2. good	_____	_____
3. red	_____	_____

4. cute _____ _____

5. bad _____ _____

6. silly _____ _____

7. much _____ _____

8. fast _____ _____

9. lovely _____ _____

10. wise _____ _____

Give yourself 10 points for A, 80 points for B, and 10 points for C. Take off 1 point for each mistake. Be sure to memorize the correct form of any adjectives on which you made mistakes.

Chapter 10

Adverbs

Just as we have adjectives which describe or modify nouns, we also have *adverbs* which describe or modify *verbs*.

Example

    The great ship sailed *slowly* out to sea.

The adverb *slowly* tells you *how* the ship sailed, just as the adjective *great* tells you more about the ship.

Adverbs are words that tell you how, when, where, or to what degree the action of the verb takes place.

Examples

    The postman got up *early*. (Tells *when* he got up.)
    He started *quickly* on his rounds. (Tells *how* he started out.)
    He walked *away* from the post office. (Tells *where* he walked.)
    She tried hard to win. (Tells *to what degree* she tried.)

Most adverbs are formed by adding *ly* to an adjective. If the adjective ends in *y*, as in *pretty*, the *y* is changed to *i* before the *ly* is added.

Examples

ADJECTIVE	ADVERB
slow	slowly
pretty	prettily
quiet	quietly
careful	carefully

Adverbs Formed from Adjectives

EXERCISE 87

Turn the adjectives below into adverbs by adding *ly*. Remember if the adjective ends with *y*, it should be changed to *i* before adding *ly*.

ADJECTIVE	ADVERB
1. loud	_____
2. bright	_____
3. high	_____
4. easy	_____
5. final	_____
6. silent	_____
7. usual	_____
8. close	_____
9. happy	_____
10. real	_____

EXERCISE 88

Diagram the following sentences and then circle as many adverbs as you can find.

Example

The man / walked (quickly.)

1. The carpenter hammered noisily._____

2. The child sang happily._____

3. The old lady spoke quietly._____

4. The priest listened silently._____

5. The woman wept sadly._____

6. The mother smiled tenderly._____

7. The baby played busily._____

8. The dog barked loudly._____

9. My teacher talks clearly._____

10. The child rubbed his eyes sleepily._____

Now go back and write beside each adverb the adjective from which it was formed.

Example

quickly   quick

EXERCISE 89

Diagram the sentences below. Circle the adverb in each one. Write the adjective from which it was formed beside it.

1. A man whistled cheerfully._____

2. The sun shone brightly._____

3. A girl sang softly to herself._____

4. The black cat purred contentedly._____

5. The radio blared loudly on the porch._____

6. The train roared noisily away.

   _____

7. A man skated rapidly across the pond._____

8. The driver shouted angrily at his son._____

9. The powerful car roared swiftly down the highway._____

10. The boat drifted lazily on the calm sea._____

Irregular Adverbs

EXERCISE 90

Not all adverbs are formed by adding *ly* to an adjective. Words such as *always, well, often, away,* and *far* are also adverbs because they tell you something about the verb. An adverb may follow or come before the verb it modifies.

Example

He (always) sits in that chair.

Always describes the verb *sits*. It tells you *when* the action of the verb takes place. Remember that adverbs usually answer *how, where,* or *when*.

Diagram each of the following sentences. Then circle the adverb and in the space provided write which of the three questions above it answers about the verb.

Example

The boy / plays the piano (well.) *How?*

1. The thief ran fast._____

2. My son always gets speeding tickets._____

3. I often run out of money._____

4. The police went away at last._____

5. The truck driver ate greedily._____

6. Tony does well at his job._____

7. My boyfriend left early._____

8. He answered quickly when I called._____

9. I see better with glasses._____

10. He traveled far from home._____

EXERCISE 91

In the sentences below, adjectives have been used incorrectly to describe the action of the verbs. Find one in each sentence and turn it into an adverb by adding *ly*.

1. The poor widow wept silent.

2. The noisy boys yell loud.

3. The men were working quiet.

4. Slow   the moon rose in the east.

5. The stars shine bright   in the sky.

6. He leaped light   over the rocks.

7. The man spoke sad   to his priest.

8. The doctor worked quick   to dress the cut.

9. He has been exercising regular.

10. The mother spoke loving   to the child.

Verb Modifiers

EXERCISE 92

The word *not* is a little adverb that modifies the verb by reversing its meaning.

Example
    Chuck did *not* come home.

Not tells how Chuck came home.

Circle all the adverbs you find in the following sentences and draw arrows to the verbs they modify. There are 12 of them. After you locate them, read the sentences again and notice what they add to their meanings.

1. My friend spoke softly to me.

2. The workers laughed merrily at the joke.

3. You have not finished your work.

4. The boy crept cautiously up the stairs.

5. They moved creakily under his weight.

6. I wish you would listen carefully to me.

7. I felt better after I took the medicine.

8. He did not like to go far from home.

9. We always eat dinner at six o'clock.

10. I often leave the office late.

EXERCISE 93

Circle all the adverbs you find in the following sentences and draw arrows to the verbs they modify.

1. The thief crept silently down the hall.

2. The phone on the table rang loudly.

3. He jumped nervously at the sound.

4. She comes frequently to my house.

5. I do not always see you in church.

6. Please do not yell loudly in the house.

7. They often take trips to the beach.

8. Al never told me about that.

9. He does not talk about other people.

10. But he always listens to them.

Comparing Adverbs

Adverbs modify verbs; they also modify other adverbs.

Example

He spoke *very* carefully.

Carefully is an adverb telling you *how* the subject spoke; *very* is an adverb modifying the adverb *carefully*.

EXERCISE 94

In the following sentences draw arrows to indicate what each adverb modifies.

Example

The dog barked very loudly.

1. The boy studied so hard for his exam.

2. She worked very carefully at her knitting.

3. Please come in more quietly.

4. She sang so sweetly that the baby stopped crying.

5. He shouted very loudly for help.

6. She criticizes more quickly than I.

7. Jack works much harder than you do.

8. I feel very well, thank you.

9. The lady spoke most kindly to him.

10. Please do not go so far from home.

An adverb can be compared by putting *more* or *most* / *less* or *least* before it.

Examples

Jim studies *more* carefully than Dick.
Mary tried *most* willingly to help me.
He drove *less* rapidly on the mountain roads.

EXERCISE 95

There are two adverbs after each sentence. Choose the appropriate one to fill in the space in each sentence. Notice how your choice changes the meaning of the other adverb it modifies.

1. John drove_____carefully after his accident. (more, less)

2. Mary is_____dependable than Jean, who is disorganized. (more, less)

3. She works_____efficiently. (most, least)

4. Please come in_____noisily. (more, less)

5. Jim spoke_____rudely after I had explained things to him. (less, more)

6. She answered me_____graciously. (most, least)

7. The doctor operated_____efficiently with good lighting. (more, less)

8. His old car travels_____rapidly than mine. (more, less)

9. She solved the problem_____intelligently. (most, least)

10. She works_____effectively when she is tired. (less, more)

Troublemakers: Good and Well

Good is an adjective and describes a noun.

Example

Mac does *good* work.

Well is an adverb and describes a verb.

Example

Mac works *well*.

Exception: *Well* is used as an adjective when referring to a person's health.

Example

How is your mother? She is *well*, thank you.

In this case, *good* and *well* do not mean the same thing. A good mother is not the same as a well mother. *Well* describes how she feels, her state of being.

EXERCISE 96

In the following sentences, fill in *good* or *well* in the blanks, depending on whether you are describing a noun or a verb.

1. Beth always behaves herself; she is a _____ girl.

2. Beth always behaves herself _____.

3. John learned his lesson _____.

4. He got a _____ mark on the test.

5. A _____ man is sometimes called a saint.

6. Nancy did her job _____.

7. That is a _____ book.

8. Jimmy's work in the shop is _____.

9. Eddie repairs cars very _____.

10. I feel very _____, thank you.

EXERCISE 97

In the following sentences using *good* and *well*, cross out the incorrect word and write in the proper one in the space provided.

Example

Jim studies ~~good~~. *well*

1. Theresa did good in school today. _____

2. Why don't you behave good? _____

3. You didn't paint good today. _____

4. He did his work goodly. _____

5. Congratulations! You spoke good in the meeting. _____

6. You learned your lesson good. _____

7. Jim did a well job. _____

8. Jenny served the guests goodly. _____

9. Miss Johnson told a well story. _____

10. Ted shoots a well game of pool. _____

Adjective Modifiers

Adverbs modify verbs and other adverbs; they also modify adjectives. Adverbs tell *how, when, where,* or *to what degree.*

Example

Ralph is a *very* good mechanic.

Good is an adjective describing mechanic. *Very* is an adverb that tells *to what degree* Ralph is good.

Some adjectives are not compared by adding *er* and *est*. In such a case, the adverbs *more* and *most* are used with the adjectives in referring to two, or to more than two, comparisons.

pretty   prettier   prettiest
beautiful   more beautiful   most beautiful

Example

Jean is *more* reliable than her sister.
She is the *most* reliable person in the class.

Diagram the following sentences. From each adverb draw an arrow to the adjective it modifies.

Example

I / am so tired.

EXERCISE 98

1. A very big dog barked at me.

2. Jimmy was always hungry.

3. May grew terribly fat.

4. My legs are always tired!

5. She looked more pleased than ever.

6. The boy grew extremely tall.

7. We are most happy about this.

8. Ted ran very fast up the hill.

9. The stranger came from a most distant land.

10. Patty was so friendly today!

EXERCISE 99

Compare the following adjectives, either by adding *er* and *est* or by putting *more* or *most* before them. Note that some words may be formed either way.

weak	_____	_____
patient	_____	_____
kind	_____	_____
delicious	_____	_____
tight	_____	_____
happy	_____	_____
fragrant	_____	_____
miserable	_____	_____
pleasant	_____	_____
careful	_____	_____

Review of Adverbs and Adjectives

Adverbs modify verbs, adjectives, and other adverbs. They answer the questions *how, when, where,* and *to what degree*.

In the following sentences, show with an arrow what word each adverb modifies. After each sentence, tell what question the adverb answers.

Example

The boy is very tall. *To what degree*?

EXERCISE 100

1. Teddy runs fast. _____

2. The child cried often. _____

3. The old man walked slowly. _____

4. The door slammed suddenly. _____

5. Her phone rang immediately. _____

6. I am very hungry. _____

7. My grandfather got too tired. _____

8. The little girl is just three. _____

9. Every day Tim grew more lonely. _____

10. The children are most excited! _____

EXERCISE 101

Adjectives modify nouns and pronouns. Adverbs modify verbs, adjectives, and other adverbs. In each sentence below, choose between the adjective and the adverb by deciding what word is being modified. Underline the correct choice.

Example
Jimmy does (careful, carefully) work.

The noun *work* is being described. Since an adjective is needed to describe a noun, the adjective *careful* is the correct choice.

Example
Jimmy works (careful, carefully).

In this sentence, the verb *works* is being modified. Therefore, the adverb *carefully* is needed.

1. The manager spoke in a (quiet, quietly) voice.

2. Joe answered him (polite, politely).

3. He comes (regular, regularly) to my house.

4. The bull was big and (strong, strongly).

5. Janie plays the guitar (good, well).

6. Davie ate his lunch (quick, quickly).

7. His wife made him a (quick, quickly) lunch.

8. I am a (slow, slowly) thinker.

9. I think very (slow, slowly).

10. Julie's embroidery is (beautiful, beautifully).

More Troublemakers

Too—an adverb with two meanings. When followed by a describing adjective or adverb, it means *too much* of anything. When set off by a comma, it means *also*.

Examples
too fat, too thin, too cold, too hastily
I want to play, too (also).

To—to do something. It is part of a verb form. It also expresses direction.

Examples
to run, to jump, to shout
to go to the station

Two—the number 2, an adjective that tells how many.

EXERCISE 102

Put the proper word (too, to, or two) in each blank space.

1. I am going _____ the park.

2. I want _____ go, _____.

3. The _____ of us will go.

4. We want _____ go _____ church.

5. It is _____ hot _____ work.

6. I have _____ sisters, _____.

7. It's _____ much trouble _____ do it.

8. This is_____ hard _____ read.

9. She's_____ busy _____ talk.

10. The apple is_____ green _____ eat.

There—an adverb meaning "in that place"; also used in sentences which start "There is" or "There are."
Their—an adjective meaning "belonging to them"; it is always followed by a noun.

Example
There is someone in there.
He is in their house.

EXERCISE 103

Put the proper word (there, their) in each blank space in these sentences.

1. _____ is too much noise in_____ room.

2. _____ office is over_____ .

3. She is in_____ club, too.

4. _____ were twenty people on_____ bus.

5. _____ house is too far away; we can't walk_____ .

6. _____ is something I don't understand about_____ behavior.

7. _____ are the men I told you about; they are over_____ .

8. I left my book on the table over_____ .

9. _____ are too many people who want _____ own way.

10. _____ is no reason for_____ critical attitude in this matter.

EXERCISE 104

Use each of the following phrases correctly in a sentence on the line below it.

Example
>   was *there*
> The teacher was there.

there is

_____

too much

_____

over there

_____

their wishes

_____

there are

_____

to go there

_____

too many

_____

to church

_____

went there

_____

their customs

_____

too hot to work

_____

their names

_____

Review Test of Adjectives and Adverbs

EXERCISE 105

A. An adjective modifies a _____ or a

_____ . An adverb modifies a _____ ,

an _____ , or another _____ . Ad-

verbs answer the questions _____ , _____ ,

_____ , and _____ _____ _____ .

B. After each of the following words, write *adj.*
or *adv.* to indicate which each one is.

kind	_____	handsome	_____
gently	_____	funny	_____
rapid	_____	lately	_____
green	_____	pretty	_____
rapidly	_____	often	_____
beautiful	_____	very	_____
good	_____	weak	_____
well	_____		

C. Diagram each of the following sentences. Draw
arrows from each adverb to the verb, adjective,
or adverb it modifies.

Example
The taxi / honked loudly in the street.

1. Dulcie walked slowly home from work.

2. She was not very happy.

3. The boss was terribly mean to her.

4. Her mother called loudly from the window.

5. She was almost late for supper.

6. She did not feel very hungry.

7. Dulcie was often lonely.

8. But tonight she felt more lonely than usual.

9. Then the telephone rang suddenly.

10. Dulcie had a very nice surprise!

D. In each of the following, tell whether the
adverb underlined modifies a verb, an adjective,
or another adverb.

Example
too tired *adj.*

1. very slowly _____

2. so heavy _____

3. worked hard _____

4. slept restlessly _____

5. much later _____

6. most wonderful _____

7. so delightfully _____

8. too heavily _____

9. studied well _____

10. too hard _____

E. After each adverb tell what question it answers: *how, when, where,* or *to what degree.*

rapidly	_____	lovingly	_____
daily	_____	often	_____
more	_____	away	_____
lately	_____	so	_____
nearby	_____	sometimes	_____

Give yourself 3 points for each sentence in C
and 2 points for all the other questions you answer
correctly. Do not count A. Take off 2 points for
each mistake. How well did you do? Be sure to
review your mistakes before going on.

Chapter 11

More Punctuation

We have already been introduced to commas, periods, and quotation marks. We have learned that a comma is used to indicate a pause and that it can change the whole meaning of a sentence.

Examples

> Don hit him.
> Don, hit him!

In the second sentence, *Don* is a noun of address, which means any name someone is called. It could be a proper name like *Don,* or it could be a term of endearment, such as *dear* or *honey*. It could also be a teasing or insulting name, such as *stupid* or *dummy*.

Example

> Look, idiot, you ought to be fired!

Here the word *idiot* is used as a noun of address and is set off from the rest of the sentence by commas before and after it.

Another use for commas is to set off a noun which follows another noun and describes it in some way. Such a noun is said to be *in apposition to* the noun it describes.

Example

> Tony, my brother, hit a home run.

Here the commas before and after *my brother* indicate that Tony is the brother spoken of. The two commas are very important. If the second one is left out, the sentence reads:

> Tony, my brother hit a home run.

This sounds as if Tony were a noun of address and that the speaker is telling Tony about the home run of another person, his brother.

Another use for commas is to indicate pauses in a series of three or more words. A series of two words requires no pause; "the fat red hen" needs no comma. But a long phrase such as "the sleek, black, elegant cat" requires two commas or one less than the number of words in the series. There is no pause between the words *elegant* and *cat*. If the sentence were turned around to read "The cat was sleek, black, and elegant," there would still be two commas after the first two of the three adjectives. There must be at least three words in a series; they must all be the same kind of words (nouns, adjectives, etc.); and there is always one comma less than there are words in the series.

These are a few of the six rules for the use of commas which you can practice in the following exercises. The rest are fairly simple or have already been introduced: for example, the use of commas to set off quotations from the rest of the sentence (review page 78).

Rules for Commas

Commas are used wherever a pause is required.

Examples
After turning off the TV, Mary went to bed.
Running to the door, he slammed it shut.

There are six common rules for using commas. Learn each one. Then put commas where they belong in the practice sentences.

RULE 1

Commas are used to separate parts of an address or a date.

Example
I live at 4 Beach Drive, Santa Monica, California.
It happened on Sunday, April 22, 1975.

EXERCISE 106

1. My birthday was last Tuesday September 9th.

2. I come from Greenfield Mass.

3. I was born on June 30 1962.

4. My grandmother lives at 4 Locust Lane Springfield.

5. Do you mean Springfield Massachusetts or Springfield Illinois?

6. Valentine's Day is on Tuesday February 14.

7. I'll be at the Hilton Hotel Los Angeles California.

8. You can reach me there until Wednesday March 18.

9. I'll be back home on Friday night March 20.

10. My address is 16 Ridge Road Arlington Virginia.

RULE 2

Words like *Oh, yes, no, well,* and *however* are set off from the rest of the sentence by commas.

Example
Oh, well, I don't care.

EXERCISE 107

1. Well shall we get started?

2. Yes it's about time we did.

3. I'm afraid however that we will be late.

4. Oh no I don't agree with you!

5. Well we shall see who is right.

6. You may however be surprised by what happens!

7. No I don't think so.

8. Well I could be wrong I suppose.

9. Yes you certainly could!

10. Oh well we'll soon find out who's right.

RULE 3

A noun of address is a name used in speaking to someone. It is set off by a comma from the rest of the sentence if it is at the beginning or end of the sentence. If it is in the middle of the sentence, it is set off by two commas, one before it and one after it.

Examples
Is that you, Ed?
Donna, your telephone is ringing.
Listen, Harry, I told you to forget it!

EXERCISE 108

1. Joe please close the door._____

2. I asked you Joe to close the door. _____

3. Honey do you like this dress on me? _____

4. Are you listening to me Peter? _____

5. Please get some ice Julie and bring it out here. _____

6. Sheila would you write that letter for me? __

7. Watch out Jim he'll bite you! _____

8. I warned you Phil to keep your dog tied up. _____

9. Darling where on earth have you been? ____

10. I've been waiting for you dear for an hour! _____

Do you remember the four kinds of sentences? In the spaces above, write what kind of sentence each one is. If you have forgotten, refer back to Chapter 5, page 45.

RULE 4

Words in a series of three or more are separated by commas. There is always one less comma than there are words in a series.

Example
My brothers are Charlie, Sandy, and Ray.

EXERCISE 109

1. Our flag is red white and blue.

2. Today we have fried chicken shrimps and spareribs.

3. My favorite sports are skating soccer and basketball.

4. The big brown hungry bear headed for the campfire.

5. Dave Ed and Joe took off hastily when they saw him.

6. The lady was hot tired and cross.

7. She had been to department stores specialty stores and discount stores.

8. She had been jostled bumped and pushed around.

9. Now all she wanted was rest peace and quiet.

10. Instead she found her children quarreling crying and fighting each other.

RULE 5

A noun next to another noun is said to be *in apposition* to it and is called an *appositive*. An *appositive* explains the first noun in some way and is set off by commas.

Example
Mr. Jones, the chairman, called the meeting to order.

EXERCISE 110

Punctuate the following sentences.

1. Millie my sister has a new dress.

2. Elizabeth II the Queen of England has four children.

3. Miss Cass I want you to meet my mother Mrs. Salerno.

4. This is my friend Ed Mahoney.

5. The lawyer Mr. Williams called us to his office.

6. Our minister Rev. Parker preached a fine sermon.

7. My father Jack Grillo is a taxi driver.

8. The captain of the baseball team Joe Murray is my pal.

9. The tiger a dangerous animal does not make a good pet.

10. Paul Tribuno the winner of the match made a short speech.

RULE 6

Commas are used to set off quotations from the rest of the sentence, except where the quotation ends in an exclamation or a question mark.

Example
"Once upon a time," began the grandmother, "there were three bears."

EXERCISE 111

In the following sentences, put in commas and quotation marks.

1. Jimmy where are you? cried the mother.

2. Jimmy she cried where are you?

3. Come here called the boss.

4. The boss called Come here!

5. Where is Kent Place? the confused driver asked.

6. Can you tell me asked the driver where Kent Place is?

7. Turn left at the next corner the policeman said. It's the first street on your right.

8. You can't miss it he added. There's a mailbox on the corner.

9. Thanks, officer said the driver for helping me out.

10. Don't mention it he replied. I'm glad to help.

Review of Commas

Commas indicate a pause and are used
1. to separate parts of addresses and dates.
2. to set off words like *yes, no,* and *however.*
3. to set off nouns of address.
4. to separate words in a series.
5. to set off appositives.
6. to set off quotations.

EXERCISE 112

Punctuate the following sentences. Whenever you use a comma, place above it the number of the rule which you are applying.

Example   6
My mother called   , "Come here, Janie."

1. Our grandmother's birthday is next Saturday February 23

2. Grandmother   how old will you be then asked Tony

3. We're having a party at her home at 129 14th Street   Cleveland Ohio

4. My mother   Mrs. Salerno   has made a big cake

5. My cousins Tony   Joe   Douglas and Mike are all invited

6. Joe   however   will not be able to come

7. Joe   I hope you are coming to the party said my mother

8. No   I can't   said Joe   I have to go
to the dentist

9. Well   come afterwards   suggested Tony

10. Yes   I could do that   said Joe
Thanks a lot Tony

Review Test of Punctuation

EXERCISE 113

Put capitals and punctuation in the following
sentences.

1. waitress can I have the meat loaf special asked

   eddie

2. it's all gone but we have stew corned beef

   and fried fish   said the waitress

3. oh nuts   said eddie   i just feel like

   having meat loaf

4. well said the waitress   how about a ham-

   burger

5. no   i had one for lunch   said eddie

6. look waitress   does the stew have dump-

   lings he asked

7. yes i think so   she answered

8. ok i'll try that   said eddie

9. here you are said the waitress   i hope you

   like it

10. thank you it hits the spot said eddie

Take off 1 point for every error. How did you
do? If you have over 80 on this test, you have a
good working knowledge of proper punctuation.
Review your mistakes before going on to the next
chapter.

Chapter 12

Prepositions

A preposition is a little word used with a noun to tell what, when, where, or how.

Example
> The men walked on the moon.

The phrase *on the moon* tells *where* the men walked. It is not a sentence because it does not express a complete thought; it has no subject and no predicate. It is simply a group of words, called a *phrase*, which contributes more information. When the phrase begins with a preposition, it is called a *prepositional phrase.*

Pre is Latin for *before* and a *preposition* is *in a position before* the noun which is its object. Previously we have discussed objects of the verb (see Chapter 2). You will recall that these are direct objects which receive the action of the verb.

Example
> Al threw the baseball.

Here, *the baseball* is the direct object which is thrown.

Example
> Al threw the baseball to Dave.

Here the prepositional phrase *to Dave* tells *where* Al threw the baseball.

Indirect Objects

Sometimes we leave out the word *to*. Then it becomes implied in the sentence.

Example
> Al threw (to) Dave the baseball.

In this case, where the preposition *to* is left out, there is no prepositional phrase. The noun *Dave* becomes the *indirect object* of the verb. The direct object is the baseball which received the action of throwing. The indirect object is Dave, to whom the ball is thrown.

There are many sentences like this in English. Often a pronoun is used as an indirect object.

Examples
> Al threw him the baseball.
> Her husband gave her some money.

To help you locate the indirect object, see if the preposition *to*, or sometimes *for*, would make sense in front of it.

Example
> The traffic cop gave (to) the driver a ticket.
> The delivery man left (for) me a package.

EXERCISE 114

Read the following sentences and underline the

indirect object in each one. It may be a noun or a pronoun. Check your work by saying "to" or "for" before each indirect object to see if it makes sense.

1. I handed Henry the letter.

2. She gave the baby his bottle.

3. The secretary took her boss the mail.

4. The man left the waiter a tip.

5. Joe got his son a new bike.

6. He gave him the bike for his birthday.

7. Will you please pass me some coffee?

8. The live wire gave him a bad shock.

9. Mrs. Gibbs told Mrs. Murphy the latest gossip.

10. I gave Mr. Kirby your message.

Now go back and circle the direct objects which receive the action of the verb.

Common Prepositions

There are many prepositions which, when combined with a noun, form prepositional phrases which explain *what*, *when*, *where*, and *how*. The noun is called the *object of the preposition*.

Examples

          (what)   (where)
A flock *of sheep* graze *in the meadow*.

          (when)   (how)
After his lunch he worked *like a beaver*.

The most common prepositions are listed below.

at	down
by	from
in	into
of	like
off	over

on	past
to	upon
up	with
for	about
above	below
across	beside
after	between
against	during
along	except
among	through
around	toward
before	underneath
behind	without

EXERCISE 115

Diagram the following sentences. In each one, circle the prepositional phrase.

Example

          The boy / sat (on the porch.)

1. Marie and Debbie ran up the steps.

2. They put their books on the table.

3. He took a box from the shelf.

4. Her sister came down the stairs.

5. She invited them into the living room.

6. They sat down on the couch.

7. We looked at a new book.

8. Later they went to the movies.

9. The toys were left on the floor.

10. She carried the dishes to the kitchen.

EXERCISE 116

For each of the phrases you circled in Exercise

115, write the little preposition and the noun which is its object in the columns below.

Example

The boy sat (on the porch.)

	PREPOSITION on	OBJECT porch
1.		
2.		
3.		
4.		
5.		
6.		
7.		
8.		
9.		
10.		

Prepositional Phrases

The different kinds of words used in our language are called *parts of speech*. We have now learned six parts of speech. Let us review them.

Part of Speech	DEFINITION
Noun	A person, place, or thing
Pronoun	Stands in place of a noun
Adjective	Describes a noun or a pronoun
Verb	Supplies the action or being in a sentence
Adverb	Describes a verb, adjective, or another adverb
Preposition	A little word with a noun as its object

A prepositional phrase is often used instead of an adjective to describe a noun. In this case it is called an *adjective phrase*.

Example

A silk dress (*silk* is an adjective)
A dress of silk (*of silk* is a prepositional phrase used as an adjective to describe the noun *dress*)

EXERCISE 117

Make up sentences using the following groups of words. These contain adjective phrases which describe nouns. Write your sentences on the line below.

1. A flock of sheep

_____

_____

2. A cap with a feather

_____

_____

3. A man in uniform

_____

_____

4. Materials for writing

_____

_____

5. A prince of royal blood

_____

_____

In each sentence you have written, circle the prepositional phrase and draw an arrow to the noun it describes or modifies. These are all adjective phrases.

Example

She wore a dress (of silk.)

A prepositional phrase is often used instead of an adverb to modify a verb, an adjective, or another adverb. This is called an *adverb phrase*.

Example

The girl ran up the stairs.

Up the stairs tells you *where* the girl ran. It modifies the verb *ran* and answers the question *where*. Thus it takes the part of an adverb.

EXERCISE 118

Make up sentences using the following groups of words. These contain adverb phrases which modify a verb. Write your sentences on the lines below.

1. jumped off the cliff

_____

_____

2. shook with laughter

_____

_____

3. waited at the gate

_____

_____

4. screamed with terror

_____

_____

5. woven by hand

_____

_____

In each sentence you have written above, circle the prepositional phrase and draw an arrow to the verb it modifies.

Review of Phrases

A preposition is a little word used with a noun to form a prepositional phrase. The phrase tells *what, when, where,* or *how.* The noun is called the object of the preposition.

EXERCISE 119

In the following sentences, circle each prepositional phrase and draw an arrow to the word it modifies.

Example

Joan played in the garden.

1. The woman waited at the door._____

2. The lamb followed the farmer to the barn.

_____

3. Julie wore a sweater of pure wool._____

4. She ran into her house._____

5. Jack rode his motorbike down the hill._____

6. Grandma's trunk is in the attic._____

7. She has a heart of gold. _____

8. Susan went through the door._____

9. The team played in the gym._____

10. The horse gallops across the meadow._____

After each phrase write *adj* or *adv*, depending on what word the preposition modifies.

EXERCISE 120

In the following sentences, circle each prepositional phrase and draw an arrow to the word it modifies.

1. A boy and a girl sat on the beach. _____

2. The girl's hair was the color of corn silk.

_____

3. The boy lay on his back._____

4. They both basked in the sunshine._____

5. The roof of my house is red._____

6. My evening dress is of white chiffon._____

7. My mother made it in the evenings._____

8. She cut it out after work._____

9. I stitched the seams on the machine._____

10. I got my wish for a long dress._____

After each phrase write *adj.* or *adv.*, depending upon what word the prepositional phrase modifies.

Analyzing Sentences

EXERCISE 121

Now you are ready to analyze sentences. This means that you can tell what each word in a sentence does—what its job is in the sentence.

Diagram the sentences below. Draw a single line under the subject and a double line under the verb. Circle all the adjectives modifying the subject. Put an *X* on all adverbs modifying the verb.

Example

The slim blonde girl / walked quickly down the street.

1. The shaggy brown dog walked slowly down the road.

2. The thin stooped man with gray hair leaned heavily on his cane.

3. A huge fat woman with a wide smile waddles cheerfully up the steps.

4. Two little boys of eight years raced noisily up the street.

5. The great golden sun rose majestically in the sky.

6. A graceful boat with white sails skims lightly over the waves.

7. The frightened cat leaped frantically for the door.

8. A crying baby wailed pathetically in the night.

9. Four workers from the farm jump quickly onto the truck.

10. The big friendly coach speaks encouragingly in the locker room.

EXERCISE 122

Now that you have shown which are the nouns and verbs and adjectives and adverbs, go back over the above sentences and see what words are left. You will find, if you have made no mistakes, that you have only prepositional phrases left. Write each phrase on the lines below. At the right write the word each one describes. Then you can tell whether it acts as an adjective or an adverb. Write *adj* or *adv* in the column on the far right.

PHRASE	WORD IT DESCRIBES	ADJ. OR ADV.
1. _____	_____	_____
2. _____	_____	_____
3. _____	_____	_____
4. _____	_____	_____
5. _____	_____	_____
6. _____	_____	_____
7. _____	_____	_____
8. _____	_____	_____
9. _____	_____	_____
10. _____	_____	_____
11. _____	_____	_____
12. _____	_____	_____
13. _____	_____	_____
14. _____	_____	_____
15. _____	_____	_____

Chapter 13

Still More Punctuation

Apostrophes

An apostrophe, for all its big name, is a little mark like a comma, except that it is placed *above* the word, as in *it's*.

Apostrophes are used *to show possession*. Coming after a singular noun, the apostrophe is followed by an *s*, as in "the girl's hair," to refer to one girl to whom the hair belongs. Since plural nouns usually end in an *s*, the apostrophe after that final *s*, as in "the girls' apartment," indicates that more than one girl owns the apartment.

When the plural form is irregular, and does not end in an *s*, as in the words we have already studied (see Chapter 2), the possessive is formed by adding an apostrophe and an *s*, just as singular possessives are formed.

Example

The man's shoe
The men's shoes

Here, the word *men* already means more than one man and does not need an *s* added to make it plural. The rule holds true for *men*, *women*, and *children*, as well as for *mice* and *geese*.

Another use for apostrophes is to indicate when parts of words are left out or contracted into a shorter form. Words such as *I'll* for *I will* or *can't* for *cannot* are called *contractions*. They are shortened by dropping out letters, and this is indicated by the use of the apostrophe. Contractions help to eliminate many long verb phrases: *Should not have* becomes *shouldn't have*. One frequently misspelled contraction is *doesn't*, short for *does not*. An irregular one is *won't*, short for *will not*. The correct contraction for *I am not* is *I'm not*, although *ain't* is frequently used in common speech.

One common contraction is *it's*, short for *it is*. It is frequently confused with *its*, which is a possessive adjective meaning *belonging to* and which is always followed by the noun it modifies.

Example

It's going to rain. (It is going to rain.)
The train jumped its track. (belonging to the train)

Other possessive adjectives include *my*, *your*, *his*, *her*, *our*, and *their*. None of them has an apostrophe, nor does *its*.

Read the examples below and do the exercises to help you understand apostrophes.

Apostrophes in Possessives

Apostrophes are used
1. to show possession.
2. for contractions.

1. The apostrophe before the *s* shows singular possession (owned by one person).

Example

That boy's work is very good.

2. The apostrophe after the *s* shows plural possession (owned by more than one).

Example
The boys' playthings were all over the floor.

3. Words which have irregular plurals that do not end in *s* are treated like singular nouns.

Example
The women's club had a meeting.

EXERCISE 123

Write the possessive for each of the following nouns and, in the blanks following them, supply something that belongs to the noun, as in the following examples.

Example

George's bicycle
The children's shoes
The dog's collar

1. Mr. Blake _____

2. The man _____

3. The girl _____

4. The girls _____

5. The lady _____

6. The ladies _____

7. The men _____

8. Father _____

9. The child _____

10. The children _____

EXERCISE 124

Punctuate the following sentences and watch for the possessives, remembering to notice whether they are singular or plural.

1. Peters book lay on the teachers desk

2. The workers mass meeting lasted a long time

3. Have you seen Joans mother she asked

4. His cars brakes were not working

5. Their cars floodlights blinded him

6. The childrens voices were too loud

7. The unions rules have to be strict

8. This is the club members project to raise money

9. Mr. Blakes house is on the hill

10. Are the womens plans completed

Apostrophes in Contractions

Apostrophes are used
1. for contractions.
2. to show possession.

Study the short or contracted form for each of the following. Note that in the negative forms using *not* the apostrophe usually stands for the *o* in *not* which is dropped. For example, *is not* becomes *isn't*.

Cross out the letters that are dropped in the left hand columns and add apostrophes to make each phrase match the contraction in the right hand column.

Example
I have   I've

I am	I'm	Where is	Where's
You are	You're	I would	I'd
He is	He's	I will	I'll
She is	She's	I have	I've
It is	It's	You have	You've
We are	We're	We will	We'll
They are	They're	What is	What's

Negative contractions

will not	won't	have not	haven't
does not	doesn't	should not	shouldn't
do not	don't	did not	didn't
can not	can't	would not	wouldn't

EXERCISE 125

Write the contractions for the following:

1. you are _____

2. do not _____

3. it is _____

4. were not _____

5. would not _____

6. can not _____

7. I am _____

8. they are _____

9. we are _____

10. I will _____

11. should not _____

12. will not _____

13. does not _____

14. he is _____

15. I have _____

16. could not _____

17. where is _____

18. I would _____

19. we will _____

20. you have _____

EXERCISE 126

In the blanks, write the contractions which could be used in the sentences.

Example
You should not do that. *shouldn't*

1. He is not ready to go yet._____

2. Do not you have dinner ready yet?_____

3. I am as hungry as a bear! _____

4. It was not a hard test._____

5. We are not going this week._____

6. I will go with you when you do go._____

7. They would not listen to directions._____

8. He does not understand English very well.

_____

9. I can not explain the lesson to him._____

10. It is a beautiful day!_____

Remember that:
isn't
hasn't } refer to one person.
wasn't

aren't
haven't } usually refer to
weren't } more than one person.

EXERCISE 127

Make up sentences using the following contractions.

1. weren't _____

2. shouldn't _____

3. I'll _____

4. wasn't _____

5. you're _____

6. don't _____

7. we're _____

8. hasn't _____

9. isn't _____

10. doesn't _____

EXERCISE 128

Use the following contractions correctly in sentences.

1. can't _____

2. haven't _____

3. they're _____

4. you've _____

5. wouldn't _____

6. you'll _____

7. I've _____

8. he's _____

9. I'm _____

10. she'll _____

Still More Troublemakers: Its and It's

Its and *it's* are often confused. The contraction for *it is* is spelled with an apostrophe, *it's*. But the possessive *its*, meaning *belonging to it*, is spelled without an apostrophe and is always followed by a noun. Whenever you use *its*, try substituting *it is* in the sentence. If it makes sense, put in the apostrophe. If it doesn't, leave it out.

Example
It's a lovely day. (It is)
The dog wagged its tail. (<u>not</u> it is)

EXERCISE 129

Change *it is* to *it's* in the following sentences by crossing out the *i* and putting in the apostrophe.

1. It is very cold.

2. It is too late now.

3. It is a beautiful day.

4. Why, it is nearly lunchtime!

5. I like it because it is funny.

6. Drink this. It is delicious!

7. Now it is time to go.

8. It is going to be such fun!

9. It is hard to spell that word.

10. It is not necessary to be rude.

EXERCISE 130

In the following sentences, put an apostrophe in *its* wherever *it is* is meant.

1. Its time to start the meeting.

2. The bus is behind its schedule.

3. Its going to take fifteen minutes.

4. The cat chased its tail.

5. Meat loses its flavor when its cooked too long.

6. Its a nice house; its lawn is lovely, too.

7. The cat carried its kittens in its mouth.

8. The chair has lost one of its legs because its so old.

9. Its going to take an hour for the train to get to its destination.

10. The dog can't find its bone because its under the refrigerator.

Colons and Semicolons

We have learned all about periods, commas, quotation marks, and apostrophes. The only punctuation marks we have not discussed are colons and semicolons.

A *colon* is two periods, one above the other like this: it is used chiefly before a list or a lengthy formal statement.

Example
> We have studied the geography of the following countries: Germany, France, Spain, Holland, Belgium, Norway.

A *semicolon* is a half-period; it is a period with a comma under it. It is used to join two short sentences together.

Example
> I called loudly; there was no answer.

EXERCISE 131

Put colons or semicolons where needed in the following sentences.

1. He crawled into the cave he looked around.

2. The teacher glanced at the clock it was nearly noon.

3. These boys made the first team Joe Ferrara, Tony Rocci, Henry Koch, Ed Argento.

4. The girl looked at him she said nothing.

5. On her grocery list were written these items apples, milk, lettuce, cereal, steak.

6. The men shouted angrily then the women screamed back at them.

7. The manager ordered the following supplies pencils, pads, carbon paper, tape, stencils.

8. Don't cry, Tommy crying won't help.

9. It was terribly hot the streets were deserted.

10. The instruments in his band were drums, a piano, a bass sax, an electric guitar, and an electric organ.

EXERCISE 132

Put all necessary punctuation in the following sentences.

1. I finished the job however I have not been paid

2. I wish to order the following four lamb chops two packages of peas one quart of milk and one head of lettuce

3. These are the books I have read this year Robinson Crusoe The Legend of Sleepy Hollow David Copperfield The Last of the Mohicans

4. My shoes are old scuffed and dirty his are brand new

5. Why O why cant I ever do anything right

6. Hear us O Lord when we cry unto Thee let our prayers be answered

7. My name is Dr J S Wilson I live at 10 Woodridge Road Chicago Ill

8. These are my favorite foods bananas peanut butter roast beef string beans and cherry pie

9. When the light turns red you stop when it is green you may go

10. The days of the week are abbreviated as follows Sun Mon Tues Wed Thurs Fri Sat

Review Test of Capitals and Punctuation

EXERCISE 133

A. Put capitals and punctuation in all *complete* sentences below.

1. after parking his car, the man

2. the boys went out to play football

3. raced across the tennis court

4. going to the window, Joan

5. opening the door quietly, the mother tiptoed into the room

6. the women gave a shower for Debbie

7. the fun began when

8. when all the presents were opened, the women

9. then they all helped to clean up

10. after the party Kathie and Sue

B. Look at the incomplete sentences. Do you know what is missing? See if you can finish the sentences so that they are complete and make sense.

C. Put capitals and punctuation where needed in the following sentences.

1. christmas day is on thursday december 25

2. oh i didnt know it comes so soon

3. well I still have to shop for my mother my father and my girl friend

4. I hope uncle oscar arrived safely

5. my friend patty has invited me to a holiday party

6. its going to be such fun she said

7. my supervisor mrs newton lives at 83 davis st greenville mass

8. her daughter carol newton is a good friend of mine

9. we were both born on aug 22 1962

10. we did not know each other however until last year

D. Put capitals and punctuation in the following sentences.

1. tony have you loaded that truck asked the boss

2. the winter months are december january and february

3. its so hot outside i had to come in

4. bless me o lord and answer my prayer

5. the letter is dated saturday sept 9 1981

6. my favorite meal is hamburgers baked beans and a glass of milk

7. our cat a siamese has blue eyes

8. its fur is long soft and fluffy

9. i called and called said the boy but nobody

answered

10. the boys voice however couldnt be heard over the radios blasting

E. Put apostrophes in the proper places.

1. girls team   6. babys bottle

2. childrens toys   7. doesnt drive

3. cant talk   8. sheeps wool

4. mens coats   9. havent got

5. ladies dresses   10. youll go

Give yourself 3 points for each sentence above and 1 point for each item in part E. Take off 1 point for each error. Be sure to review anything that gives you trouble before you go on.

Chapter 14

Conjunctions and Interjections

The last two parts of speech that we have to learn are *conjunctions* and *interjections*.

The hardest things about these little words are their names. That's because they're based on Latin; so naturally they are harder for us than English. Now let's learn a little Latin!

Con means *with,* and *junction* means *joined—joined with.* A junction is a station where different railroad lines connect. Just as two railroad lines connect at the junction, so two sentences are connected by conjunctions. *And* is the most commonly used conjunction. Subjects connected by *and* are called *compound subjects* (see Chapter 1). In the same way, sentences connected by *and* are called *compound sentences.*

Example
(Compound subject)   (Compound sentence)
Mary *and* Jane shopped *and* then they went home.

An injection is a shot. What do we say when we get a shot? *Ouch! Ow! Eek! Wow!* and maybe *Whew!* when it is over. These words are all *interjections. Inter* means *into* or *between* and *jection* means *shot.* They are shot into the sentence to express strong feeling. Usually they stand alone, though sometimes they are actually between *(inter)* the words of the sentence.

Example
Nuts! I forgot my lunch!
I fear, alas, that all is lost.
Hear us, O Lord, when we cry to Thee.

Conjunctions

Conjunctions are bridge words. They join words and sentences together the way a bridge connects islands. The conjunctions most frequently used are

> and but
> or because
> so for

A conjunction may connect
1) nouns in a compound subject.

Example
Susan *and* Gladys are there.

2) verbs in a compound predicate.

Example
The cheerleaders yelled *and* shouted.

3) Two separate sentences in a compound sentence.

Example
Tom / rang the bell, *and* my brother / opened the door.

EXERCISE 134

Separate these compound sentences into two parts and draw a line between them. Circle all the conjunctions. You should be able to find ten of them.

Example

He went home /(and)called up his friend.

1. My parents love me but they get angry at me.

2. Do your work well or you will be fired.

3. He missed his train, for his taxi was caught in heavy traffic.

4. Jim wanted a new bike but he couldn't afford one.

5. The next Friday was his birthday so his father bought one for him.

6. We went to the clambake and Charlie ate at least ninety clams.

7. I like the meat but I don't want the vegetables.

8. You must practice hard or you won't do well.

9. We waited a long time, for Hal was late.

10. Then the door opened and he walked in.

EXERCISE 135

In each line below are two short sentences. Rewrite them, using the conjunction that follows the end of the sentence to make one smooth sentence instead of two short, choppy ones.

Example

The baby cried. His mother came. *so*

The baby cried so his mother came.

1. I am late. I lost my way. *because*

_____

_____

2. You go now. I'll come later. *and*

_____

3. The game was over. I went home. *so*

_____

_____

4. The bell rang. No one answered it. *but*

_____

_____

5. Mary ran to the door. She knew who was there! *for*

_____

_____

6. Mrs. Smith took the inventory. Then she ordered more supplies. *and*

_____

_____

7. Debbie baked a pie. They would have dessert. *so*

_____

_____

8. Get out of here. Don't come back. *and*

_____

_____

9. It didn't hurt at first. Later it hurt a lot. *but*

_____

_____

10. I couldn't do my homework. I didn't have time. *because*

_____

_____

Interjections

EXERCISE 136

Interjections are the Lone Rangers of our language. They stand alone, usually separated by an exclamation mark. They modify nothing and have no job in the sentence except to express strong feeling or excitement as in *Oh!*, *Ouch!*, and *Wow!* *Oh* is sometimes spelled without the *h* when used with a noun of address.

Example
Hear us, O Lord, when we cry unto Thee.
Wow! Look at that!

Underline the interjections in the sentences below.

1. "Bah and humbug!" said Scrooge.
2. Lo, a miracle happened!
3. Oh, my! I almost forgot!
4. Nuts! I should have known better.
5. Whew! That was a narrow escape!
6. Alas, we must say farewell.
7. Hurray! We won the lottery!
8. Hey, wait for me!
9. Have mercy upon us, O Lord!
10. Ouch! I cut my finger!

EXERCISE 137

Put capitals and punctuation in the following sentences.

1. my goodness i forgot my dental appointment
2. hey where do you think youre going
3. good lord whats going on here
4. hear my prayer o lord and be merciful
5. pow robert hit the crook hard
6. ding dong the bells are ringing
7. gee whiz thats not fair
8. the boy fired his toy gun bang and the bird flew away
9. boy you made a strike
10. we won hurray for our team

Review of Prepositions, Conjunctions, and Interjections

EXERCISE 138

What part of speech is followed by a noun, forming a phrase?_____

What part of speech expresses excitement or emotion?_____

What part of speech joins words and groups of words in a sentence?_____

Diagram the following sentences; notice that some are compound sentences. Circle each prepositional phrase and draw an arrow to the word it modifies.

1. The police in the patrol car drove down the road.
2. Ouch! I caught my finger in the door!
3. Pete and Dave fished in the river.
4. The girls on the stage sang and danced before the audience.
5. The food was very hot, but it was tasty.
6. The foreman was very strict in the factory.

7. On the street, though, he laughed and fooled with the workers.

8. I took my brother to the circus on his birthday.

9. Gee, we ate lots of popcorn, for it was delicious!

10. I liked all the animals, but the elephants were the best in the show.

From the sentences above, select two examples of each of the following and write them in the spaces provided.

1. Prepositional phrases used as adjectives.

_____

_____

2. Prepositional phrases used as adverbs.

_____

_____

3. Interjections._____ _____

4. Conjunctions used with compound subjects and predicates._____ _____

5. Conjunctions used to join two complete sentences._____ _____

Review

We have now learned all the eight parts of speech used in our language. Let us review them.

Noun—refers to a person, place, or thing, including things you cannot touch such as *love* or *anger*. Times and seasons such as *noon, Tuesday,* or *autumn* are also nouns.

Pronoun—stands in place of a noun and refers back to it.

Verb—expresses action or being

Adjective—describes a noun or a pronoun.

Adverb—describes a verb, an adjective, or another adverb.

Preposition—forms a phrase with the noun which is its object.

Conjunction—joins words or sentences together.

Interjection—expresses excitement or emotion.

Sometimes the same word may be used in different ways. You have to decide what function a word has in a sentence before you can name what part of speech it is.

Examples

Her mother packed her summer clothes.

(*Summer* is an adjective describing the noun *clothes.*)

Summer is my favorite season of the year.

(In this sentence, *summer* is a noun, the subject of the sentence.)

His *work* is very difficult.

(Here, *work* is a noun, the subject of the sentence.)

They *work* all day in the fields.

(In this case, *work* is a verb expressing action.)

Parts of Speech

EXERCISE 139

Read the following sentences carefully. It may help to diagram them. The underlined words serve different functions in different sentences. After each sentence write what part of speech the underlined word is in that particular sentence.

1. I love my children. _____

2. Love is a wonderful feeling._____

3. The children taste the new dessert._____

4. My sister has good taste in clothes._____

5. My mattress has a broken spring._____

6. All the flowers bloom in the spring._____

7. The kids <u>spring</u> on the trampoline._____

8. We went to a <u>dance</u> last night._____

9. They <u>dance</u> well together._____

10. I would enjoy his <u>talk</u> if he didn't <u>talk</u> so much._____

9. Roger put the money in his <u>pants</u> pocket.

_____

10. The dog <u>pants</u> for water because he is hot.

_____

EXERCISE 140

After each sentence write what part of speech the underlined word is in that particular sentence.

1. I played with him during the <u>noon</u> recess.

_____

2. My mother came home at <u>noon</u>._____

3. The dog <u>barks</u> at the child._____

4. His <u>bark</u> is worse than his bite._____

5. The <u>ring</u> of the bell woke Jerry._____

6. Please <u>ring</u> for the nurse._____

7. My shirt is made of <u>cotton</u>._____

8. Janet wore a new <u>cotton</u> dress._____

A Reminding Rhyme

You have learned what each word in a sentence is and what its job is in making a complete sentence. The rhyme below will help you remember what you have learned.

A *noun's* a person, place, or thing,
Or sometimes even time, like spring.
A *verb* tells what the subject does,
Like "jumps" or "fishes," "is" or "was."
An *adjective* describes a noun,
Like "gay" or "ugly," "rich" or "brown."
An *adverb* tells you how or when,
Like "quietly" or "well" or "then."
A *pronoun* takes the noun's own place,
Like "they" for "children," "she" for "Grace."
A *preposition* leads a noun:
"In bed," "at sea," or "to the town."
Conjunctions are a bridge across
Two sentences: "but," "and," "because."
The *interjections,* last of all,
Like "Oh!" and "Ouch!" are very small.

Chapter 15

Letter Writing

Letters are very important in our society. We write friendly letters to our friends and family and business letters to companies about various matters. A well-written letter should express the writer's thoughts clearly. This chapter contains good examples of both friendly and business letters.

There are differences in style between friendly and business letters. Study the models below before you compose your own. You have already learned the use of capitals and commas in punctuation; note, however, that no periods are used in the heading of a letter.

Friendly Letter

Heading———►   3 Rutland Road
                 Great Neck, N. Y. 11405
                 Dec. 11, 19———

Greeting———► Dear Dave,

    It has been a long time since I've seen you. In all this ice and snow, last summer seems very far away. But I haven't forgotten what a good time we had.

Body

    My Christmas vacation begins next week, on December 18. Why don't you come and visit me? Bring your skates because the ice is perfect now. If it snows again, we can go to New Hampshire for a day or two of skiing.

    Please write soon, and tell me that you'll come. We could have a great time.

Closing———►   Always your friend,
Signature———►   Joe

Heading: This is the writer's address and the date on which the letter was written. Often the writer's address is printed on his stationery, in which case only the date needs to be written in the upper right-hand corner.

Greeting: This depends on the relationship between the writers. The writer might begin "My dear Aunt Sally" or "Dear Miss Neary." The first word is capitalized, as is the name of the person written to. The greeting may be followed by either a comma or a colon, but in friendly letters commas are used more often.

Body: A handwritten letter should be indented at the beginning of each paragraph. A margin of about an inch should be left on the left-hand side to make the letter look neat and evenly spaced.

Closing: This is indented about halfway across the page and is followed by a comma. Its wording also depends on the writer's mood and relationship to his correspondent. The closing might read, "With love," "Affectionately," "Lovingly," "Always yours," or just "Yours." To someone who is not a close friend or relative, the closing would read "Yours truly," "Yours sincerely," or "Very truly yours," just as in a formal business letter.

Signature: This should be centered beneath the closing and may consist of just the writer's first name or his full name, depending on how well he knows the person to whom he is writing. You would not, of course, sign your full name when writing to your parents or to your girl friend. The signature should always be handwritten, whether the letter is written or typed.

An envelope should be addressed in the lower right-hand quarter, if the spacing permits. The longer the address, of course, the further toward the left it will have to begin. The writer's address should be in the upper left-hand corner. The stamp should be neatly placed in the upper right-hand corner.

J. Wiley, Jr.
3 Rutland Rd.
Great Neck, N.Y. 11405

Mr. David Williams
42 Locust Ave.
Gloversville
New York 12735

Envelopes for business letters are addressed in the same way. The title of the person to whom you are writing is given, if you know it, followed by the name of the firm. The writer's return address should always be in the upper left-hand corner.

J. Wiley, Jr.   stamp
3 Rutland Rd.
Great Neck, N.Y. 11405

Mr. John M. Williams, President
Creative Concerns, Inc.
549 Fifth Ave.
New York, N.Y. 10016

Business Letter

Business letters are usually typed in single space, with inch-wide margins. Between paragraphs, leave two spaces. The paragraphs and closing are indented the same as in a friendly letter. Recently, however, many business firms have been using a newer form without indentations. A sample of this modern style is shown in the letter below. In either case, the letter is signed by hand above the typewritten signature, so be sure to leave four spaces after the closing before typing the signature.

The following is a sample business letter:

3290 49th Avenue
Rome, Ohio 10035
July 29, 19——

Acme Electronic Company
1479 Davis Street
St. Louis, Texas 10029

Dear Sir:

On June 10 I ordered pocket calculator #SB-47763-4 from your catalog, but an error was made in the shipment I received. The pocket calculator that was sent to me was #SB-47765-2, which I am returning to you. Please send me the pocket calculator that I originally ordered. Thank you for your cooperation.

Yours truly,

Carl Gutterman

Heading: In a business letter from a private person, the heading is typed on the right as in a friendly letter.

Greeting: The greeting is preceded by the formal name and address of the firm to whom the letter is written. If the letter is written to a specific person, his name is given first. The greeting is formal: "Gentlemen:" or "Dear Sir:" or "Dear Madam:" is appropriate.

Body: The body of the letter is brief and to the point. If you are writing to order merchandise, always state clearly the model, number, and price of the items ordered. Allow enough for postage and taxes, and specify how you want the goods shipped. If you are writing to complain about poor merchandise received, be sure to give all the above information and your order number.

Closing: This is formal and does not vary much. "Yours truly," "Yours sincerely," or "Very truly yours" are standard closings.

Signature: The signature is handwritten above the typed signature; leave four spaces between the closing and the typed signature.

Job Application Letter

There are several important things to remember when writing a job application letter. First, your letter should be brief and should follow the format of a regular business letter. If you are answering an advertisement that appeared in a newspaper or magazine, be sure to state exactly where and when you saw the ad. Next, give your prospective employer some information about yourself, for example, your educational background and your previous work experience. Also, list any skills you have that would be useful for the particular job you're interested in. Finally, tell your prospective employer how he or she can get in touch with you for an interview. The following is an example of a job application letter:

> 1042 Dayton Avenue
> Kansas City, Kansas 67911
> December 3, 19——

Director of Personnel
Randall Advertising Agency, Inc.
1405 Harcross Boulevard
Kansas City, Kansas 67932

Dear Sir:

I am writing in response to your advertisement for a receptionist which appeared in the November 29th issue of the *Kansas City Star*.

I am a recent high school graduate and am very interested in the advertising field. Because I enjoy working with people, I feel that I could perform the duties of a receptionist well. I would like the opportunity to put into practice the business procedures and typing skills I learned while in school.

I am available for an interview at your convenience. You may reach me between 9:00 A.M. and 5:00 P.M. at 967-2931. I look forward to hearing from you.

> Sincerely,
>
> *Jane Gray*
>
> Jane Gray

Notice that the style of this letter is direct and to the point. The writer tells what skills and qualities she has to offer her prospective employer. She also states how she can be reached during the day. If you have any previous work experience, be sure to describe it briefly and give references with telephone numbers where possible. Good luck!

Chapter 16

Final Review

EXERCISE 141

A. Do you remember the four kinds of sentences? After each sentence write the initial for the kind of sentence it is. If in doubt review Chapter 5.

1. What a beautiful day! _____

2. It's too nice to stay inside. _____

3. Go on out and get some exercise. _____

4. Don't you want to go out? _____

5. I'll help you with your homework later. _____

6. What are you waiting for? _____

7. Help me carry these packages. _____
    _____

8. What's the matter? Don't you feel well? ____
    _____

9. Quick, call a doctor! _____

10. I knew something was wrong. _____

B. Put capitals and punctuation where needed in the following sentences.

1. peter david and jeff are brothers

2. they live at 35 spring st houston tex

3. peter the oldest was born on Apr 21 1965

4. jimmy will you please come here called his friend

5. i cant now joe shouted jimmy im right in the middle of this

6. its all right said his friend i found what i wanted

7. the minister rev carey came into the room

8. she put the camera back in its case

9. mens shoes and ladies hats are on the fifth floor

10. o lord what am i going to do now she sighed

C. In the following sentences, write the correct word in the blank space.

1. We went to_____ house for dinner. (their, there)

2. Betsy has done her work _____. (good, well)

3. It's_____cold_____go outside. (too, to, two)

4. _____ are some good books here but this one is the _____. (their, there; better, best)

5. Doris grows more _____ every day. (lovely, lovelier)

More Final Review

EXERCISE 142

Diagram the following sentences. Remember the subject of an imperative sentence is implied (you).

1. Oh, the needles and pins are in my workbox.

2. Mr. Baldwin, the president, came into the office.

3. The clerks listened very quietly to him.

4. He lectured and scolded them.

5. A flock of geese flew over the trees.

6. The dark leaden sky was heavy with rain.

7. Joe, please pass the bread.

8. Jerry is the strongest boy on the team.

9. High in the sky the sun shone.

10. There is Mrs. Kaufman, our neighbor.

From the sentences above, choose and give examples of the following:

1. A singular common noun _____

2. A plural common noun _____

3. A proper noun _____

4. A compound subject _____

5. A compound verb _____

6. A predicate noun _____

7. A noun of address _____

8. An appositive noun _____

9. A collective noun _____

10. A verb of being, present tense _____

11. A verb of action, past tense _____

12. A direct object _____

13. A predicate adjective _____

14. A pronoun as subject _____

15. A pronoun as object _____

16. A prepositional phrase modifying a noun _____ _____

17. An adverb modifying a verb _____

18. An adverb modifying another adverb _____

19. An interjection _____

20. A conjunction _____

21. A prepositional phrase modifying a verb _____

22. Give the present tense of *flew* _____

23. Give the present tense of *shone* _____

24. Give the "most" form of an adjective _____

25. Give an irregular plural noun _____

Final Test

EXERCISE 143

A. Put capitals and punctuation in the following sentences.

1. pete are you going to the baseball game asked ted

2. who wants to watch the mets lose again said pete

3. oh well said ted its better than staying home watching television

4. tomorrow is my birthday i was born on tues aug 31 1955

5. when i was small we lived in chicago at 151 spring st

6. my uncles car hasnt a spare tire

7. dr spencer came to dinner on thanksgiving day

8. my boss mr j f morris doesnt take any nonsense

9. bobbys little brothers are jimmy arthur and dick

10. the boys bats and mitts lay all over the porch

B. Correct any incomplete or run-on sentences. Add words or punctuation if necessary. After each sentence write the initial for the kind of sentence it is.

1. I washed the dishes and made the beds then I vacuumed the rug._____

2. What a lot of work you did!_____

3. Did your mother thank you?_____

4. Stop making so much noise._____

5. When I was ready for school _____

C. Diagram each of the following sentences.

1. The Pope gave his blessing to the crowd.

2. The dog in the last kennel barks loudly.

3. The family spent Labor Day at their grand-mother's house.

4. Up the quiet street skipped Julie and Judy, the twins.

5. They laughed and chattered merrily.

6. Their mother called them but they skipped on.

7. We are the two fastest runners on the track team.

8. The boy in the corner is very tall.

9. Millie wants us to go with her.

10. But we are much too busy.

D. From the sentences above, select and write on the space below an example of

1. A proper noun_____

2. A common singular noun_____

3. A collective noun_____

4. A noun used as a direct object_____

5. A plural pronoun used as a subject_____

6. A pronoun used as an object_____

7. An adverb modifying a verb_____

8. An adjective modifying a noun_____

9. A predicate nominative_____

10. A compound sentence (give its number)

_____

11. A compound subject_____

12. A compound verb_____

13. A verb of being in the present tense_____

14. A verb of action in the present tense_____

15. A prepositional phrase used as an adjective_____

16. A prepositional phrase used as an adverb

_____

17. A predicate adjective_____

18. A noun in apposition_____

19. An adverb modifying an adjective_____

20. A conjunction_____

E. Give the plurals of

1. policeman_____

2. family_____

3. leaf_____

4. noise_____

5. mouse_____

F. Give the present tense of

1. gave_____

2. spent_____

3. was_____

4. sang_____

5. chattered_____

G. Compare the following adjectives.

Adjective	More	Most
1. proud		
2. good		
3. beautiful		
4. merry		
5. bad		

H. Write a different pronoun as a subject for each of the following verbs.

1. _____ am

2. _____ are

3. _____ is

4. _____ was

5. _____ were

Scoring: Give 3 points for each sentence in A.
Give 2 points for each sentence in B and C.
Give 1 point for each item in D, E, F, G, and H.
Take off 1 point for each mistake.

If you have over 80 points on this test, you have a good basic understanding of correct English. It will help you to speak and write more effectively. Be sure to correct your mistakes, going back to read the instructions if there is anything you still don't understand.

Conclusions

We have come to the end of a long road. We began with the simplest of two-word sentences, gradually building up an understanding of long compound sentences with perhaps two or three subjects or verbs. We have studied all eight parts of speech so that you understand what function each one performs in the construction of a sentence.

As we explained in the Introduction, English is a very complicated language which has come down to us from ancient sources. There are many more irregularities and complicated forms than we have been able to cover in this book. In some cases we have overlooked exceptions to the rules, and we have simplified more difficult subjects, such as compound verb forms. But with this basic knowledge as an introduction, you can go on and increase your knowledge further if you wish to.

This has been hard work, but you will find it has been worth the effort. If you have done the work well, you should now have a much better understanding of how to construct good simple English sentences. You can have confidence in your ability to communicate clearly and correctly. This will help you in your day-to-day work and give you more enjoyment in your communications with others. May the efforts you put into this work bring you success and satisfaction.

M. A. P.

Answer Key for Exercises

EXERCISE 1

1. Fish / swim. [S/P]
2. Bees / buzz. [S/P]
3. Birds / fly. [S/P]
4. Babies / cry. [S/P]
5. Cats / purr. [S/P]
6. Trains / run. [S/P]
7. Planes / fly. [S/P]
8. Boats / sail. [S/P]
9. Wood / burns. [S/P]
10. Children / play. [S/P]

EXERCISE 2

1. The snow / fell. [S/P]
2. A flower / bloomed. [S/P]
3. The girl / cried. [S/P]
4. The food / smelled good. [S/P]
5. A boy / yelled. [S/P]
6. The car / speeds by. [S/P]

7. The man / whistled softly. [S/P]
8. A girl / laughed. [S/P]
9. The bells / rang loudly. [S/P]
10. The clock / struck ten. [S/P]

EXERCISE 3

1. The boys played baseball.
2. A dog barked far away.
3. The car speeded past.
4. A policeman stopped it.
5. The driver looked unhappy.
6. The ticket cost him ten dollars.
7. An apple rolled off the table.
8. The women shopped for bargains.
9. Jimmy loves to fish.
10. An eagle soared across the sky.

EXERCISE 4

1. The clouds gathered in the east.
2. A plane roared overhead.

109

3. The <u>flowers</u> wilted without water.

4. The <u>telephone</u> rang for a long time.

5. An <u>ostrich</u> has long legs.

6. The <u>traffic</u> grew much heavier.

7. <u>Alice</u> danced around the room.

8. An <u>umbrella</u> keeps off the rain.

9. The <u>students</u> did their homework.

10. A <u>lady</u> wrote to her son.

Check your answer key carefully. Did you find all the subjects correctly? How many subjects were preceded by *a*? **2** How many by *an*? **2** Write the vowels at the beginnings of the words preceded by *an*. **o, u**

EXERCISE 5
(Suggested Subjects)

1. *The girl* /<u>walked</u> into the pizza parlor.

2. *The man* /<u>handed</u> out hundred dollar bills.

3. *The dog* /<u>growled</u> furiously outside the door.

4. *A cat* /<u>chased</u> the frightened child.

5. *The child* /<u>sits</u> under a tree and dreams.

6. *The thief* /<u>drove</u> a big blue Cadillac.

7. *The shovel* /<u>dug</u> deep into the soft earth.

8. *The clown* /<u>wore</u> a crazy flowered hat.

9. *An actor* /<u>stalked</u> across the empty stage.

10. *The man* /<u>shouted</u> angrily at the boy.

The	*A*	*An*
8	**1**	**1**

EXERCISE 6

1. The <u>boy</u> /<u>dialed</u> the wrong number.

2. The <u>painter</u> /<u>fell</u> off the ladder.

3. The <u>chef</u> /<u>prepares</u> a delicious meal.

4. The <u>family</u> /<u>ate</u> dinner at the new restaurant.

5. A <u>dog</u> /<u>chases</u> a squirrel in the park.

6. An <u>artist</u> /<u>drew</u> a sketch of the old bridge.

7. The <u>elephant</u> /<u>escapes</u> from the zoo.

8. An <u>apple</u> /<u>falls</u> from the tree.

9. The <u>dentist</u> /<u>filled</u> the cavity quickly.

10. The <u>elevator</u> /<u>stopped</u> on the tenth floor.

EXERCISE 7
(Suggested Predicates)

1. The hairy <u>monster</u> /*attacked the village*.

2. An <u>astronaut</u> /*walked on the moon*.

3. The fat old <u>lady</u> /*ate the pizza*.

4. A green sports <u>car</u> /*turned the corner*.

5. The husky <u>policeman</u> /*wrote a ticket*.

6. My <u>grandmother</u> /*bakes cookies*.

7. The tall <u>waiter</u> /*served dinner*.

8. The girl's blonde <u>hair</u> /*looked fake*.

9. The frightened <u>horse</u> /*reared*.

10. The baseball <u>team</u> /*won the game*.

EXERCISE 8

Every sentence must have:
1. A subject which performs the action. It is called a *noun*.
2. A predicate which describes the action the subject does. The main word is a *verb*.

1. Frank / whistled.
2. The birds / sang.
3. The employees / ate lunch.
4. Our team / won.
5. Mary / fed her cat.
6. Joe / dropped his hammer.
7. The clock / stopped.
8. A bell / rang.
9. The sun / shone in the sky.
10. Flowers / blossom in spring.
11. The moon / rose across the lake.
12. The canoe / glided down the river.
13. The red car / roared down the street.
14. Ed / hit the ball hard.
15. The boys / played a game.
16. The passengers / lined up quickly.
17. The supervisor / handed out the paychecks.
18. The big black dog / chased me away.
19. The goldfish / swims around the pond.
20. The shining stars / gleam in the sky.

4. Babies / cry when they are hungry.
5. Cats / purr deep down in their throats.
6. Trains / run from Boston to California.
7. Planes / fly very low over the airport.
8. Boats / sail up and down the lake.
9. Plants / need sunlight and water.
10. Children / play in the park.

EXERCISE 10

1. The snow / fell three feet deep last night.
2. A red flower / bloomed in her garden.
3. The girl / cried because she couldn't go.
4. The food / smelled good to the hungry men.
5. A boy / yelled at the big bully.
6. The foreign car / speeds by with the police after it.
7. The man / whistled softly to himself.
8. A girl / laughed at his joke.
9. The church bells / rang loudly on Sunday morning.
10. The clock / struck ten in the empty old house.

EXERCISE 9

1. Fish / swim all over the lake.
2. Bees / buzz around the flowers all day.
3. Birds / fly south in the winter.

EXERCISE 11

1. The big gray cat / sat on the fence.
2. Thick white snowflakes / drifted down.
3. A very tall boy / ran across the street.

4. A big red car/roared down the highway.

5. A police car/speeded after it.

6. A fat old lady/rocked the baby.

7. The shouting boys/skated in the park.

8. A sleepy old man/opened the door.

9. Two tired children/crawled into bed.

10. The red-headed girl/spells very well.

EXERCISE 12

2. telephone 7. street

3. team 8. dog

5. house 10. hero

7. car 10. day

1. The young actor/combed his hair.

2. My sister/answered the telephone.

3. Our football team/beat the other team.

4. Our coach/praised our good playing.

5. The silent thief/sneaked into the house.

6. The big watchdog/barked at him.

7. A policeman/drove his car up the street.

8. The sneaky thief/ran away from the dog.

9. The policeman/grabbed him as he ran.

10. The watchdog/became the hero of the day.

EXERCISE 13

1. Rachel and Bill/took a taxi home.

2. The audience/cheers and claps for the actor.

3. Mike, Tom, and Betsy/organized the meeting.

4. The young man/slips and falls on the ice.

5. The car and the bike/collided at the light.

6. The guests/laugh and dance at the party.

7. Nancy and her sister/left early.

8. They/bought groceries and cooked dinner.

9. Mary/opened the door and walked into the room.

10. Steve and his girl friend/had an argument.

EXERCISE 14
(Suggested Answers)

1. Beth and Jane _went shopping_.

2. Ships and airplanes _hasten travel_.

3. Dogs and cats _often fight_.

4. Thunder and lightning _frightened her_.

5. Men and women _enjoy tennis_.

Write sentences using the following *compound predicates:*

1. _The girl_ danced and sang.

2. _The boys_ run and jump.

3. _The wrestler_ struggled and sweated.

4. _The children_ told jokes and played games.

5. _Jim_ jumped into the water and swam.

EXERCISE 15

1. The frightened kitten/crawled under the bed. (S P)
2. The cross old lady/scolded the waiter. (s P)
3. Torn yellow curtains/hung in the window. (S P)
4. The winter wind/shrieked and howled down the alley. (S P)
5. Robins and bluejays/sat in a tree. (CS P)
6. The excited brown puppy/ran around barking. (S P)
7. A beautiful girl/bought the white satin dress. (S P)
8. The fat little boy and his brother/ate the whole cake. (CS P)
9. A train/whistled loudly. (S P)
10. The train/roared into the station. (S P)
11. The shining moon/rose over the city. (S P)
12. A cherry tree/bloomed in the park. (S P)
13. The winter rain/poured down on the earth. (S P)
14. The thin man/hurried down the street. (s P)
15. The angry dogs/growled and barked at the stranger. (s CP)
16. The hungry fish/swim toward the bait. (S P)
17. The warm spring sun/shone brightly. (S P)
18. The red sports car/roared up the hill. (S P)
19. The very exciting game/ended finally. (S P)
20. The noisy boys/shouted and cheered. (S CP)

EXERCISE 16

1. The cat/chased a mouse. (S P O)
2. His mother/called Tom. (S P O)
3. My sister/wore my dress. (S P O)
4. The policeman/grabbed the thief. (S P O)
5. The firemen/stopped the fire. (S P O)
6. His car/hit a tree. (S P O)
7. The teacher/graded the papers. (S P O)
8. The mother/rocked the baby. (S P O)
9. The man/paid his bill. (S P O)
10. The wind/rattles the windows. (S P O)

EXERCISE 17

1. The dog/gnawed his bone. (S P O)
2. A bird/sang a song. (s P O)
3. The farmer/planted seed. (S P O)
4. Snow/covered the ground. (S P O)
5. The ship/hit a reef. (S P O)
6. The waves/pounded the rocks. (S P O)
7. A jet plane/broke the sound barrier. (S P O)
8. The capsule/hit the ocean. (S P O)
9. The rocket/missed its target. (S P O)
10. A bomb/shattered the building. (S P O)

EXERCISE 18

1. Julie asked her mother for a quarter. (X X)
2. The fish swam around the pond. (X X)

3. (Jonah) was swallowed by a whale. [X]

4. The little yellow bird sang in the tree. [X X]

5. (June) is my favorite month. [X]

6. (Robert) moved to (California.)

7. His father bought a house in (Los Angeles.) [X X]

8. The picture fell off the wall. [X X]

9. (Mary) asked (Grandmother) to read her a story. [X]

10. The dog bit the mailman. [X X]

EXERCISE 19

1. (Patty) has a brother named (David.) [X]

2. A little white rabbit ran across the yard. [X X]

3. (Central Park) is in (New York.)

4. (Mary) answered the telephone. [X]

5. The children were going to school. [X X]

6. (Don) plays for the (Mets.)

7. (Abe) hit the ball with a stick. [X X]

8. The cheerful cook baked a big chocolate cake for (Christmas Day.) [X X]

9. My favorite sports are football, tennis, and track. [X X X x]

10. (George,) (Joe,) and (Tony) have parts in a show on (Broadway.)

EXERCISE 20

1. The girl bought a hat in the store. [XS XS XS]

2. The families of the (Canadians) waited at the airport. [XP P XS]

3. The boys played ball with (Billy.) [XP XS S]

4. My home is in (Chicago,) but I have a bungalow on (Lake Erie.) [XS S S XS]

5. (Betty) dropped a dish on the floor of the restaurant. [S XS XS XS]

6. My cat chased (Fido) across the grass and down (Elm Street.) [XS S XS S]

7. On (Sunday) the fellows went to (Shea Stadium.) [S XP S]

8. The wolves howl on the mountains on cold winter nights. [XP XP XP]

9. (John) and his brother assembled the (Volkswagen.) [S XS S]

10. Those boys belong to (Little League.) [XP S]

EXERCISE 21

1. (George Washington) was our first president. [S XS]

2. (Mark Twain) and (Washington Irving) are famous American writers. [S S XP]

3. The (Amazon) is the longest river in (South America.) [S XS S]

4. The (Giants) won the game with the (Jets) last Saturday. [P XS P S]

5. Sons often grow up to be like their fathers. [XP XP]

6. There are many pink flowers on the cherry tree. [XP XS]

7. One tulip bloomed in my garden. [XS XS]

8. (Jupiter) is a planet with several moons.

9. (Venus) and (Mars) are also planets.

10. We had beef and potatoes for dinner.

EXERCISE 22

1. toy   *toys*

2. body   *bodies*

3. guy   *guys*

4. lady   *ladies*

5. fly   *flies*

6. party   *parties*

7. sky   *skies*

8. key   *keys*

9. hobby   *hobbies*

10. story   *stories*

EXERCISE 23

1. chimney   *chimneys*

2. company   *companies*

3. valley   *valleys*

4. pony   *ponies*

5. ray   *rays*

6. bunny   *bunnies*

7. family   *families*

8. delay   *delays*

9. monkey   *monkeys*

10. candy   *candies*

EXERCISE 24

1. trio   *trios*

2. tomato   *tomatoes*

3. rodeo   *rodeos*

4. piano   *pianos*

5. photo   *photos*

6. igloo   *igloos*

7. embargo   *embargoes*

8. auto   *autos*

9. cargo   *cargoes*

10. hero   *heroes*

EXERCISE 25

1. A *herd* of cows grazed in the meadow.

2. A *flock* of chickens was in the yard.

3. A *group, class* of children played in the park.

4. The United States *Army* trains its officers at West Point.

5. The *audience* in the theater enjoyed the show.

6. The *congregation* of the church attended Sunday services.

7. A *gang, bunch, group* of boys gathered on the street.

8. A *grove* of pine trees grew in the valley.

9. Our baseball *team* won the game.

10. My Boy Scout *troop* went on a hike.

EXERCISE 26

1. thieves   *thief*

2. women   *woman*

3. houses   *house*

4. mice   *mouse*

5. armies   *army*

6. nations   *nation*

7. pianos   *piano*

8. boxes   *box*

9. children   *child*

10. nurses   *nurse*

11. leaves   *leaf*

12. tomatoes   *tomato*

13. teeth   *tooth*

14. cabbages   *cabbage*

15. horses   *horse*

16. hobbies   *hobby*

17. lice   *louse*

18. knives   *knife*

19. knees   *knee*

20. laces   *lace*

EXERCISE 27

A noun is the name of a *person*, *place*, or *thing*.

1. Sally / wears (slacks) to work.
    S   P

2. The bird / carried a (worm) to its nest.
      S   P

3. Frank and Mario / raced their (cars) down the highway.
    CS   P

4. A policeman / drove his (motorcycle) after them.
    S   P

5. The tall trooper / gave a (ticket) to each of them.
    S   P

6. A flock of ducks / waddled across the road.
    S   P

7. Sandy and Liz / enjoyed the (movie.)
    CS   P

8. The children / jumped and ran in the playground.
    S   P   CP

9. The sun / rose from behind the mountains.
    S   P

10. The American army / won the (battle.)
    S   P

Any five of the following are correct.

PROPER NOUNS

Sally   *Sandy*

Frank   *Liz*

Mario

COMMON NOUNS

1. *slacks*
2. *bird, worm, nest*
3. *cars, highway*
4. *policeman, motorcycle*
5. *trooper, ticket*
6. *flock, ducks, road*
7. *movie*
8. *children, playground*
9. *sun, mountains*
10. *army, battle*

SINGULAR NOUNS	PLURAL NOUNS
All proper nouns plus bird, worm, nest, highway, policeman, motorcycle, trooper	*slacks, cars, ducks, children mountains*

ticket, flock, road,

movie, playground,

sun, army, battle

1. A compound subject _includes more than one noun_.

2. A compound predicate _includes more than one verb_.

3. A collective noun _is singular in form but it includes a number of people or things_.

Diagram the following sentences as usual. Put a circle around any objects.

1. A robin | built its (nest) in the tree.
   S   P

2. The Bermans and the Shaws | live in Chicago.
              CS   P

3. Julie and Pam | led the (parade.)
   CS   P

4. The crowd | shouted and screamed.
       S   CP

5. Our team | won three football (games.)
       S   P

6. A gang of boys | broke (windows) in the school.
       S   P

7. A policeman | caught and arrested the (fellows.)
       S   CP

8. Our club | elected a (president) named Joe Ferrara.
       S   P

9. The astronauts | walked in outer space.
       S   P

10. The rocket | reached the (moon) safely.
        S   P

COMPOUND SUBJECT

Bermans and Shaws

Julie and Pam

COMPOUND PREDICATE

shouted and screamed

caught and arrested

COLLECTIVE NOUNS

gang, team, club, crowd

PROPER	COMMON	SINGULAR	PLURAL
Bermans	robin	robin	Bermans
Shaws	nest	nest	Shaws
Chicago	tree	tree	games
Julie	parade	Chicago	windows
Pam	crowd	Julie	fellows
Joe Ferrara	team	Pam	astronauts
games	parade		
gang	crowd		
boys	team		
windows	gang		
school	school		
policeman	policeman		
fellows	club		
club	president		
president	Joe Ferrara		
astronauts	space		
space	rocket		
rocket	moon		
moon			

EXERCISE 28

1. Bill chased _me_ into the house. (I, me)

2. _I_ began to scream for my mother. (I, Me)

3. _She_ came running when she heard. (She, Her)

4. Joe and Harry came home for dinner with _me_ . (I, me)

5. My mother cooked a turkey for _them_ . (they, them)

6. After dinner _we_ all watched TV. (we, us)

7. Do you want to come with _us_ ? (we, us)

8. _We_ are going to a show. (We, Us)

9. _She_ was wearing a new dress. (She, Her)

10. It looked beautiful on _her_ . (she, her)

EXERCISE 29

1. Polly and _I_ went swimming. (I, me)

2. _He_ and Mary went to the movies. (He, Him)

3. They went with my boy friend and _me_ . (I, me)

4. Either Dan or _I_ will pick you up. (I, me)

5. You can go with _us_ if you want. (we, us)

6. _He_ and _I_ are buddies. (He, Him; I, me)

7. That's secret between you and _me_ . (I, me)

8. They have an agreement among _them_ . (they, them)

9. Both _she_ and _I_ were late to school. (she, her; I, me)

10. Was there a quarrel between _her_ (she, her) and _him_ ? (he, him)

EXERCISE 30

PRESENT TENSE	PAST TENSE
1. skate	_skated_
2. study	_studied_
3. buzz	_buzzed_
4. bloom	_bloomed_
5. whistle	_whistled_
6. light	_lighted_
7. laugh	_laughed_
8. cry	_cried_
9. marry	_married_
10. wash	_washed_

EXERCISE 31

PRESENT TENSE	PAST TENSE
1. _wish_	wished
2. _ask_	asked
3. _like_	liked
4. _try_	tried
5. _drop_	dropped
6. _plant_	planted
7. _wash_	washed

8. _note_   noted

9. _chase_   chased

10. _provide_   provided

EXERCISE 32

1. raise   He _raises_
2. dress   She _dresses_
3. hate   He _hates_
4. brush   She _brushes_
5. fry   He _fries_
6. smile   She _smiles_
7. want   He _wants_
8. carry   She _carries_
9. push   It _pushes_
10. wait   He _waits_

1. raises   _raised_
2. dresses   _dressed_
3. hates   _hated_
4. brushes   _brushed_
5. fries   _fried_
6. smiles   _smiled_
7. wants   _wanted_
8. pushes   _pushed_
9. waits   _waited_
10. carries   _carried_

EXERCISE 33

1. _waits_   He waited.
2. _requires_   It required.
3. _rushes_   She rushed.
4. _demands_   He demanded.
5. _cries_   She cried.
6. _screams_   He screamed.
7. _mates_   It mated.
8. _kills_   He killed.
9. _moves_   It moved.
10. _fires_   He fired.

EXERCISE 34

PRESENT	PAST
1. take	_took_
2. run	_ran_
3. eat	_ate_
4. go	_went_
5. come	_came_
6. grow	_grew_
7. speak	_spoke_
8. fight	_fought_
9. hit	_hit_
10. fall	_fell_
11. fly	_flew_
12. swim	_swam_
13. tell	_told_

14. sing   _sang_
15. make   _made_
16. rise   _rose_
17. shine   _shone_
18. win   _won_
19. feed   _fed_
20. drink   _drank_

EXERCISE 35

1. _writes_   wrote
2. _wins_   won
3. _shoots_   shot
4. _comes_   came
5. _goes_   went
6. _sits_   sat
7. _breaks_   broke
8. _rises_   rose
9. _swims_   swam
10. _buys_   bought
11. _shines_   shone
12. _sleeps_   slept
13. _tells_   told
14. _lights_   lit
15. _catches_   caught
16. _bends_   bent
17. _feeds_   fed
18. _holds_   held

19. _takes_   took
20. _thinks_   thought

EXERCISE 36

1. Celeste/is a pretty girl.
2. The dog/was black and white.
3. I/am hungry for supper.
4. The men/are outdoors.
5. The train/was late tonight.
6. The stars/were bright in the sky.
7. This horse/is very smart.
8. The audience/was too noisy.
9. I/am glad to see my friend.
10. The women/were in the office.

EXERCISE 37

1. Richie __is__ the best pitcher.
2. Jim and Doug __are__ catchers on our team.
3. Julie Andrews __was__ the star in *Mary Poppins.*
4. At night I __am__ sleepy.
5. You think you __are__ so smart!
6. Yesterday you __were__ late to work.
7. Last summer Tim __was__ working.
8. Now he __is__ back in school.
9. This week my brother __is__ home on leave from the army.

10. Where _are_ you going tomorrow?

10. He *was* a very good coach all that year.

EXERCISE 38

    S P
1. She/was very mean to me.

     S   P
2. They/are not nice to strangers.

        S P
3. Our family/is together on weekends.

   S P
4. We/were at the beach last Sunday.

       S   P
5. The weather/was very hot.

   S P
6. It/was almost too hot to walk on the sand.

      S   P
7. The waves/were very powerful.

          S   P
8. Sometimes people/are not very thoughtful.

     S   P
9. They/were often at home.

   S P
10. I/am pleased with your progress.

1. _She_   4. _It_

2. _They_   5. _They_

3. _We_   6. _I_

EXERCISE 39

1. I *am* hungry.

2. He *is* my brother.

3. The boys *are* members of the baseball team.

4. Last year they *were* the high school champions.

5. She *is* the best student in the class.

6. We *are or were* very good friends.

7. We *were* watching TV at my house last night.

8. My mother *is* going out shopping.

9. Last year our coach *was* Chuck Wilson.

EXERCISE 40

                 P S
1. In the last row sits/John. _Pr._

                        P   S
2. At the back of the room was/a huge fireplace. _P._

                   P   S
3. Under my window grows/a beautiful rose-bush. _Pr._

                           P
4. On the porch in a rocking chair sat/the old, old lady. _P._

                            P
5. After all the cold weather comes/the warm, lovely spring. _Pr._

                P   S
6. Next to my house is/a little park. _Pr._

               P   S
7. Down the chimney came/Santa Claus! _P._

             P   S
8. After the dinner came/a delicious dessert. _P._

                  P   S
9. Inside all the tissue paper was/a tiny gold box. _P._

                         P   S
10. Last of all, after everybody else, came/Peter! _P._

EXERCISE 41

                       S   P
1. Next to the wall the children/planted (flowers.)

                     S   P
2. With great caution the robber/opened the (window.)

                         P   S
3. Under the trees in the shade sat/the old man.

                    S   P
4. With a terrible roar, the jet/passed overhead.

                S   P
5. After lunch the brothers/went shopping.

          P   S
6. Last of all comes/the grand prize.

            S P
7. On Saturday we/took a (trip) to Connecticut.

8. Barking angrily, the dog/charged the (stranger).
   (S P O)

9. Smiling sweetly, the lady/opened the (door) for
   (S P)

   the guests.

10. After the storm came/the sunshine again.
    (P S)

7. They/ built their house themselves.
   (S P O)

8. Bruce/ feeds his cat three times a day.
   (S P O)

9. You/are an excellent writer.
   (S P PN)

10. I/ am the best cook in my family.
    (S P PN)

EXERCISE 42

1. The boys/caught a fish.
   (S P O)

2. My grandmother/is Mrs. Wilson.
   (S P PN)

3. Jimmy/hit a foul ball.
   (S P O)

4. Mary/is the oldest person here.
   (S P PN)

5. I/am your new supervisor.
   (S P PN)

6. The boy/slammed the door.
   (S P O)

7. You/are the last one to finish.
   (S P PN)

8. Joe/carried the garbage can outside.
   (S P O)

9. Tom/shoveled the driveway for me.
   (S P O)

10. The students/ did their work quickly.
    (S P O)

EXERCISE 43

Follow the same directions as for Exercise 42.

1. John/is a good friend of mine.
   (S P PN)

2. He/opened the package from his sister.
   (S P O)

3. Janet/ left her purse at home.
   (S P O)

4. That desk/is an antique.
   (S P PN)

5. We/gave a party for the couple.
   (S P O)

6. She/is a reporter for the local newspaper.
   (S P PN)

EXERCISE 44

	PRESENT	PAST
1.	wash	washed
2.	fill	filled
3.	twist	twisted
4.	dress	dressed
5.	choke	choked
6.	mend	mended
7.	rain	rained
8.	land	landed
9.	mail	mailed
10.	test	tested

1.	am
2.	are
3.	is
4.	was
5.	were

EXERCISE 45

	PRESENT			PAST
1. I	am		7. He	was

2. She _is_   8. I _was_

3. You _are_   9. We _were_

4. We _are_   10. She _was_

5. They _are_   11. You _were_

6. It _is_   12. They _were_

EXERCISE 46

PRESENT	PAST
1. dig	_dug_
2. run	_ran_
3. sing	_sang_
4. think	_thought_
5. fly	_flew_
6. sit	_sat_
7. drink	_drank_
8. win	_won_
9. bring	_brought_
10. sink	_sank_

(Suggested Verbs)

11. _is_	_was_
12. _go_	_went_
13. _speak_	_spoke_
14. _eat_	_ate_

EXERCISE 47

1. First we eat breakfast and then we ~~went~~ to school. _(go)_

2. Mary cut Anne's hair and curls it. _(ed)_

3. The mother fed and changes the baby. _(d)_

4. You wash the dishes and I dried them. _(y)_

5. We ate and ~~drink~~ well. _(drank)_

6. The boys fight and yelled at each other.

7. The policeman stops his car and walked over to the boys. _(s)_

8. The fire engine roared down the street and ~~skids~~ around the corner. _(skidded)_

9. I went to the movies and then I ~~come~~ home. _(came)_

10. I am in a hurry but he ~~was~~ not. _(is)_

EXERCISE 48

A. 1. The three boys/fished all day in the river. _(S) (P)_

2. Bass, pickerel, and trout/were their catch. _(CS) (P)_

3. Low in the sky sank/the sun. _(P) (S)_

4. The evening shadows/crept across the valley. _(S) (P)_

5. Home went/the boys with their catch. _(P) (S)_

6. Their supper that night/was delicious fresh fish. _(S) (P)_

7. Tim, Jack, and Joe/were old friends. _(CS) (P)_

8. They often/went fishing together. _(S) (P)_

9. One day they/saw a school of pickerel. _(S) (P)_

10. Now they/watch the river every day. _(S) (P)_

B. 1. A proper noun _Jim, Jack, Joe_

2. A common singular noun _day, river, bass, pickerel, etc. etc._

3. A collective noun _school_

4. A verb of being _were, was_

5. A verb of action in the past tense _fished, sank, crept, went_

6. A direct object _school, river_

7. A compound subject _Jim, Jack, and Joe_

8. A pronoun _They_

9. A verb in the present tense _watch_

10. A predicate noun _catch, fish, friends_

	SINGULAR	PLURAL
C. 1.	woman	_women_
2.	lady	_ladies_
3.	boy	_boys_
4.	wish	_wishes_
5.	gentleman	_gentlemen_
6.	_mouse_	mice
7.	_house_	houses
8.	_goose_	geese
9.	_day_	days
10.	_knife_	knives

	PRESENT	PAST
D. 1.	wash	_washed_
2.	go	_went_
3.	fly	_flew_

4.	sing	_sang_
5.	think	_thought_
6.	am	_was_
7.	want	_wanted_
8.	creep	_crept_
9.	watch	_watched_
10.	run	_ran_
11.	_wander_	wandered
12.	_ring_	rang
13.	_buy_	bought
14.	_are_	were
15.	_swim_	swam
16.	_stop_	stopped
17.	_is_	was
18.	_belong_	belonged
19.	_wear_	wore
20.	_blossom_	blossomed

E. 1.	_I_	am
2.	_He, She, It_	was
3.	_you, we, they_	were
4.	_you, we, they_	are
5.	_He, She, it_	is

F. 1. Yesterday he _was_ here.

2. Tomorrow I _am_ going home.

3. They _were_ at the picnic last week.

4. She *is* the happiest person I know.

5. We *are* leaving right now.

EXERCISE 49

1. What do you want ? Q

2. I want to go with you. S

3. Jim hit John. S

4. Why did he do that ? Q

5. It was not John's fault. S

6. Jim has a nasty temper. S

7. Where are you going ? Q

8. I am going to work. S

9. Do you like your boss ? Q

10. No, he is too crabby. S

How many questions did you find? 4

EXERCISE 50

1. What shall we do now ? Q

2. Shall we go fishing ? Q

3. No, I don't feel like fishing. S

4. Would you like some ice cream ? Q

5. This is good, isn't it ? Q

6. Tomorrow is my day off. S

7. What will you do ? Q

8. I hope it doesn't rain. S

9. I have to paint the house. S

10. Wouldn't you like to help me ? Q

EXERCISE 51

1. Go on home now. C

2. Oh! I forgot something! E

3. Turn off the headlights. C

4. Quick! Call the police! E or C

5. Please shut the door. C

6. Don't walk on the grass. C

7. Hey! Guess what happened! E or C

8. Call me up tonight. C

9. Long live the king! E

10. Please pass in your papers. C

EXERCISE 52

1. *you* Hand me that book. C

2. Hear this. Now *you* hear this. C

3. What a wonderful idea! E

4. Gee, that would be great! E

5. Please *you* tell me what happened. C

6. It's a deep, dark secret! E

7. *you* Turn right at the corner. C

8. Holy cow, look at that! E or C

9. *you* Get a move on, you guys. C

10. *you* Get going before you get caught. C

EXERCISE 53

1. What time is it? Q

2. Drop that gun. _C_

3. George was late to work. _S_

4. Nina, come here at once. _C_

5. Don't you think Patty reads well? _Q_

6. The telephone rang for a long time. _S_

7. How fast the children ran! _E_

8. Please put it on the table. _C_

9. May I borrow that book? _Q_

10. Joe needs another pencil. _S_

EXERCISE 54

1. Come in, please. _C_

2. Why are you late? _Q_

3. Quick, call a doctor. _C_

4. That is a pretty dress. _S_

5. Do you like it? _Q_

6. I think it's lovely! _E_

7. It is time for lunch. _S_

8. Do you like to swim? _Q_

9. Close that window. _C_

10. It's a beautiful day. _S_

EXERCISE 55

A   1. What kind of sentence ends with a question mark? _Question_

2. What kind of sentence makes a statement of fact? _Statement_

3. What kind of sentence has an implied subject *You*? _Command_

4. What kind of sentence expresses excitement? _Exclamation_

5. What must every sentence begin with? _Capital_

B 1. P please pass the butter. _C_

2. W why are you so late ? _Q_

3. I it is much colder tonight. _S_

4. M my goodness, what a surprise! _E_

5. W what happened ? _Q_

6. S somebody got hurt. _S_

7. G gosh, that's terrible! _E_

8. D did you call a doctor ? _Q_

9. H help, call the police! _E or C_

10. T they're already here. _S_

C 1. W what time is it ? _Q_

2. I it is seven o'clock. _S_

3. P pass the bread, please. _C_

4. I it is time for bed. _S_

5. G get to bed, boys. _C_

6. Henry broke his leg. _S_

7. H how did he do that ? _Q_

8. Q quick, get a doctor! _E or C_

9. G get Dr. Fox on the telephone. _C_

10. H he's coming right over. _S_

W
11. what are you doing ? Q _____

d
12. it's none of your business . S _____

d
13. don't get fresh with me . C _____

a
14. are you looking for trouble ? Q _____

d
15. gosh, you must be nuts ! E _____

W
16. why don't you get lost ? Q _____

17. I have a sore throat . S _____

g
18. get out of the way . C _____

d
19. do you think you can win ? Q _____

20. ouch, that hurt ! E _____

EXERCISE 56

1. ~~went down the street~~
a
2. two girls went down the street.
a
3. they waited on the corner.

4. ~~running down the path~~

5. ~~when she went in the house~~

6. ~~suddenly a voice~~
d
7. suddenly Nancy heard a voice.

8. ~~in the gray light of dawn~~
a
9. the boys went fishing.

10. ~~and ran to the window~~

How many complete sentences did you find? 4

EXERCISE 57

1. ~~three cars are~~
a
2. three cars are colliding.

3. ~~the cop on the corner~~
a
4. the cop on the corner has a gun.

5. ~~after my lunch~~
d
6. soon the bell rang.

7. ~~turned on the light~~
m
8. my mother turned on the light.

9. ~~when the doorbell rang~~
w
10. when the doorbell rang I opened the door.

EXERCISE 58
(Suggested Sentences)

1. when the siren sounded

When the siren sounded I jumped.

2. rushing downstairs, Sally

Rushing downstairs, Sally tripped.

3. Norman said that he

Norman said that he would do his homework.

4. and sat down to watch TV

He had a snack and sat down to watch TV.

5. on a hot summer day

On a hot summer day you can find the family at the pool.

6. like to swim

I like to swim.

7. John and Bill also

John and Bill also like to play golf.

8. rang again and again

    The telephone rang again and again.

9. up the ladder

    He climbed up the ladder to fix the roof.

10. later in the day

    The reception was held later in the day.

EXERCISE 59
(Suggested Sentences)

1. ran into the house

    She picked up the kitten and ran into the house.

2. the lamp on the table

    The lamp on the table is a new one.

3. my lunch at work

    I always eat my lunch at work.

4. I wish I had taken

    I wish I had taken my mother's advice.

5. too cold to go

    It was too cold to go swimming.

6. right after breakfast

    Right after breakfast I did the dishes.

7. standing quietly in the corner

    The boy was found standing quietly in the corner.

8. their friends and relatives

    Their friends and relatives attended the wedding.

9. before dark

    Her mother said she had to be home before dark.

10. it was very

    It was very generous of them to lend us the money.

EXERCISE 60

1. Your letter came yesterday. I read it. Afterwards I showed it to my buddy.

2. His umbrella blew away in the wind. It went flying down the street.

3. The cat was angry. She started clawing me. Then I hit her.

4. My wife asked me to go to the store. I forgot all about it.

5. Someone called my name. I turned around. There was my friend Joe.

6. I read about him in the paper. It said he was a great pitcher.

7. Jim wanted to go to the movies. His girl friend wanted to go dancing.

8. A big plane was flying over the house. Suddenly we heard an explosion. We ran outside.

9. All we could see was dust. Then suddenly flames sprang up.

10. People were screaming. I tried to get close. The flames were too hot.

EXERCISE 61

1. *a* after the show we went to the drugstore.*w*e each had a Coke.

2. *y*esterday was my mother's birthday. I forgot to buy her a present.

3. *H*e heard a noise.*I*t was outside his window.

4. *W*hen she left work it was raining.*S*he took a taxi home.

5. *I*t's too cold in here.I think I'll get my sweater.

6. *M*y brother asked me to drive him to work.I couldn't because my car was being repaired.

7. *L*ast night we came home late.*W*e got caught in a traffic jam.

8. I wish I had a bike.*T*hen I could ride to work.

9. *S*he starts her new job this week.I hope she likes it.

10. *M*aybe they will visit us soon.*W*e enjoy their company

How many sentences did you find? __20__

EXERCISE 62

A   1. What is a sentence?
___It expresses a complete thought.___

2. What are the two parts of a sentence?
___Subject and Predicate___

3. What must a sentence begin with?
___Capital letter___

4. What must a sentence end with?
___Punctuation (or period)___

5. What is a run-on sentence?
___Separate sentences strung together___

B   1. *W*here are you going, my pretty maid ?

2. ~~after we go to the show~~

3. I would like a drink of water.

4. *H*e went to work.*T*hen he came home for dinner.

5. ~~because it is so hot~~

6. *F*irst she wrote the report,*a*fter that she went to the meeting.

7. *A*fter all that, she was tired out.

8. *H*e's a big tall guy with red hair.

9. ~~although he gets his work done~~

10. *F*irst he did setting-up exercises.*T*hen he took a hot shower.

(Suggested Sentences)

C   1. my father and I
___My father and I often go to the ball games.___

2. where did you
___Where did you go when you left the house?___

3. the planet Mars
___The planet Mars is the red planet.___

4. oh, my goodness

Oh, my goodness, I forgot my car keys!

5. ran faster than ever

Our horse ran faster than ever at this morning's race.

6. why were they

"Why were they late?" asked the teacher.

7. the people in our car pool

The people in our car pool gave Joe a surprise birthday party.

8. out of the window

By looking out of the window, I can see the New York skyline.

9. fell flat on his face

He slipped on the pavement and fell flat on his face.

10. the teacher's dress

The teacher's dress was very stylish.

11. when did she

When did she have the baby?

12. the fellows in this block

The fellows in this block all belong to the same club.

13. ran down the street

The thief ran down the street and was caught.

14. with the siren screaming

With the siren screaming, the police car turned the corner.

15. good heavens

Good heavens, look at that!

16. what is that

What is that dance called?

17. the last thing

What is the last thing you remember?

18. did he ask

Did he ask you if he could borrow the car?

19. out the window

The canary flew out the window.

20. why in the world

Why in the world would you want to do that?

EXERCISE 63

1. The supervisor said, "Let's start our meeting."

2. Alex announced, "Our new cleaning products are very popular."

3. Mary stated, "We made a large profit from them in the first six months."

4. Susan remarked, "They sell best in the Middle West."

5. Bill replied, "That's where we have done the most advertising."

6. Mary suggested, "We need more radio ads in other parts of the country."

7. Alex said, "It's important to find out why our customers prefer our products."

8. Susan said, "Let's make a survey of our customers in the Middle West."

9. Bill answered, "That's a great idea."

10. The supervisor said, "Now we'll discuss those radio ads."

EXERCISE 64

1. Sarah announced, "I'd like to go camping for our vacation."

2. Bob said, "That's impossible because we don't have any camping equipment."

3. Sarah answered, "We could borrow the Nelsons' equipment."

4. Bob said, "OK, but we need to decide where we're going."

5. Sarah suggested, "I think Ontario would be a lovely place to camp."

6. Bob sighed, "Yes, but that would be a long drive."

7. Sarah replied, "Well, we could camp along the way."

8. Bob said, "But we have only two weeks of vacation."

9. Sarah said, "I guess that isn't enough time."

10. Bob suggested, "We could camp at one of the state parks near here."

EXERCISE 65

1. "I got a raise," announced Sally at dinner.

2. "I'm very pleased to hear it!" exclaimed her mother.

3. "You've worked very hard for that," said her father.

4. "I think this calls for a celebration," he added.

5. "I think so, too," Sally's mother said.

6. "I don't see anything so great about it," growled her brother.

7. "That's just because you're jealous," snapped back Sally.

8. "Now don't quarrel at dinner," said their mother.

9. "I was going to suggest a treat for all of us,"

10. "In that case, it's OK with me," announced Sally's brother.

EXERCISE 66

1. "I'd like to go camping for our vacation," Sarah announced.

2. Bob said, "That's impossible because we don't have any camping equipment."

3. "We could borrow the Nelsons' equipment," Sarah answered.

4. Bob said, "OK, but we need to decide where we're going."

5. Sarah suggested, "I think Ontario would be a lovely place to camp."

6. "Yes, but that would be a long drive," Bob sighed.

7. Sarah replied, "Well, we could camp along the way."

8. "But we have only two weeks of vacation," Bob said.

9. Sarah said, "I guess that isn't enough time."

10. "We could camp at one of the state parks near here," Bob suggested.

EXERCISE 67

1. "Where are you going?" asked the young woman.

2. "I'm going running," answered the young man.

3. "Can I come with you?" she asked.

4. "Of course you can!" he exclaimed.

5. "I like having company when I run," he added.

6. "Oh, and I love the exercise," said the young woman.

7. "When did you start running?" asked the young man.

8. "I started about two years ago," she said.

9. "I wanted to keep in shape," she added.

10. "Come on, let's go," he said.

EXERCISE 68

1. "Where am I?" asked the bearded man.

2. "You are in the hospital," said the nurse.

3. "The hospital! Good heavens!" exclaimed the man.

4. "Now, don't get excited," the nurse said. "We will take good care of you."

5. "What happened to me?" asked the man.

6. "You were hit by a car," said the nurse. "Don't you remember anything?"

7. "I remember riding my motorcycle," the man said. "I don't know what happened after that."

8. "Am I going to get well?" he asked.

9. "Of course you are!" exclaimed the nurse. "The doctor will soon be here."

10. "Thank goodness for that," sighed the man.

EXERCISE 69

A 1. Where on earth have you been ? Q

2. Heavens, you had me worried to death! E

3. Don't you ever run off like that again. C

4. I was afraid you had been run over. S

5. Why didn't you telephone me ? Q

6. I would have come and picked you up. S

7. Listen to me when I'm talking to you. C

8. You are simply impossible. S

9. You owe me an explanation. S

10. Good gracious, she's running away again!

B 1. "Where are you going?" asked the police officer.

2. "I'm not telling," the little boy said.

3. The police officer looked at him and asked, "What's your name?"

4. "I won't tell you," answered the boy.

5. "Does your mother know you're out?" asked the officer.

6. The little boy muttered, "No."

7. "Don't you think she'll worry?" the officer said.

8. "She won't care," said the little boy.

9. "Here comes a lady now," said the officer.

10. "Billy, where have you been?" the lady cried. "You had me worried sick."

EXERCISE 70

1. This is the first day of October.

2. Tom and Dick both live in Springfield.

3. S star light, star bright,

   F first star I see tonight.

4. M marie and E ellen live in P pittsburgh.

5. T thank you for the book you sent me for

   C christmas.

6. S should old acquaintance be forgot and

   never brought to mind?

   S should old acquaintance be forgot and

   days of auld lang syne?

7. C columbus discovered A america on O october

   12, 1492.

8. R rick brought K katie to the party.

9. T there is a zoo in C central P park in the middle of

   N new Y york C city.

10. G george W washington lived in M mt. V vernon,

   V virginia.

EXERCISE 71

1. M my birthday is on S saturday, O october 23.

2. J joe's birthday is the next day, S sunday.

3. J joe and V victor are my best friends.

4. T the P president of the U united S states lives in the

   W white H house.

5. R roses are red, violets are blue,

   S sugar is sweet and so are you.

6. I love C christmas even better than T thanksgiving.

7. C columbia U university is in N new Y york C city.

8. D dr. F fisher is our family doctor.

9. N near us is the C coliseum.

10. M my country, 'tis of thee,

   S sweet land of liberty,

   O of thee I sing.

EXERCISE 72

1. O give thanks unto the L lord for H he is good.

2. I wish I had a new F ford.

3. M my father reads The the D daily N news.

4. O oh nuts, I forgot my lunch!

5. W why, O why, am I so stupid?

6. The the W wind in the W willows is a good book.

7. S show me T thy ways, O lord; teach me T thy

   paths.

8. H have you read The the A adventures of T tom

   S sawyer?

9. M my composition is called the the F first P president

   of the U united S states.

10. The the L lord is my shepherd; I shall not want.

THE DAFFODILS

I wandered lonely as a cloud

T that floats on high o'er vales and hills,

W when all at once I saw a crowd,

A host of golden daffodils,

B beside the lake, beneath the trees,

F fluttering and dancing in the breeze.

William Wordsworth

EXERCISE 73

1. my name is joseph w wiley.

2. i live at 3 rutland rd. in great neck, n y.

3. the ship is commanded by capt. peter smith.

4. the director of the f b i lives in washington, d c

5. gen. johnson commands the armed forces of

   the u s a

6. i got a b s degree from city college.

7. rev. keating lives at 35 w. fourteenth st, n y c

8. mr. and mrs. j. williams, jr. live at 19 lynn rd.,

   springdale, mass,

9. samuel schulman, m d has an office in the

   medical bldg.

10. his office hours begin at 10 a m

EXERCISE 74

1. P. M.   *Afternoon (Post Meridian)*

2. F. B. I.   *Federal Bureau of Investigation*

3. B. C.   *Before Christ*

4. A. D.   *Anno Domini*

5. U. N.   *United Nations*

6. P. O.   *Post Office*

7. U. S. A.   *United States of America*

8. N. Y. C.   *New York City*

9. M. D.   *Medical Doctor*

10. A. M.   *Morning (Ante Meridian)*

EXERCISE 75

1. thomas jefferson wrote the declaration of

   independence.

2. george washington was our first president.

3. abraham lincoln composed the gettysburg

   address.

4. the battle of bunker hill began the american

   revolution.

5. the liberty bell is in a museum in philadelphia.

6. the empire state building used to be the tallest

   building in the world.

7. radio city is at 49th st. and fifth ave. in new

   york.

8. the mississippi river flows into the gulf of

   mexico.

9. hawaii and alaska are our newest states.

10. children believe santa claus lives at the north

    pole.

EXERCISE 76

1. Street   *St.*

2. Road   *Rd.*

3. January   *Jan.*

4. December   *Dec.*

5. Monday   *Mon.*

6. Tuesday   *Tues.*

7. Wednesday   *Wed.*

8. October   *Oct.*

9. Nebraska   *Neb. or NE*

10. Connecticut   *Conn. or CT*

11. Thursday   *Thurs.*

12. February   *Feb.*

13. Massachusetts   *Mass. or MA*

14. Friday   *Fri.*

15. November   *Nov.*

16. Mountain   *Mt.*

17. Doctor   *Dr.*

18. Professor   *Prof.*

19. Saturday   *Sat.*

20. General   *Gen.*

EXERCISE 77

A. 1. george, elvis, and john have a rock group,
the weirdos.

2. thanksgiving day comes on november 22
this year.

3. dr. anderson lives in mt. hermon, mass.

4. hear me, oh lord, when I pray unto thee.

5. julie's father is in the f.b.i.

6. prof. dennis teaches at columbia university.

7. the name of my book is a tale of two cities.

8. saturday is my favorite day of the week.

9. I will send your package c.o.d. to 231 main
st. springfield, mass.

10. sing a song of seasons,

something bright in all,

flowers in the summer,

fires in the fall!

B. 1. "where are you going?" asked my brother.

2. "out to play baseball," I answered.

3. he shouted after me, "hey, can I come?"

4. "oh I guess so," I said.

5. we headed down main street toward prospect
park.

6. dr. j.j. robbins works at the dallas city hospital.

7. corp. g. steward lives at 10 main st. denver, col.

8. judy said she would be home by 12 p.m.

9. she didn't come until 2 a.m.

10. boys flying kites haul in their white-winged
birds,

you can't do that way when you're flying
words.

thoughts unexpressed may sometimes fall
back dead,

but god himself can't change them once
they're said.

Will Carlton

EXERCISE 78

1. The (slim,)(long-haired) girl /waited on a (busy)
corner.

2. She /wore a (pink) shirt and (ragged) (blue) jeans.

3. My (new) car /has (bucket) seats and (red) upholstery.

4. The (big) (brown) dog /chased the (frightened) thief.
   - S over dog, P over chased

5. The (brightest) girl on our block /is (little) Beth.
   - S over girl, P over is

6. The (big) (black) cat /sat in the (sunny) window of the (grocery) store.
   - S over cat, P over sat

7. On (cold) (winter) nights I /like a (blazing) fire.
   - S over I, P over like

8. The (icy) wind /blows (stinging) snow down the (narrow) streets.
   - S over wind, P over blows

9. But in our (cheerful) kitchen is /a (warm) stove.
   - P over is, S over stove

10. His (plump) (rosy) mother /hums an (old) (Italian) song while she cooks (delicious) lasagna.
    - S over mother, P over hums

EXERCISE 79

(Suggested Adjectives)

1. The _young_ girls giggled as the _handsome_ boys walked by.

2. A _tall_ skyscraper is being built overlooking the _picturesque_ bay.

3. A _stiff_ breeze blew in from the _stormy_ ocean.

4. He drove his _red_ convertible down the _lonely_ highway.

5. A _large_ basket of flowers stood on the _picnic_ table.

6. A _young_ girl rode on the _small_ bicycle.

7. The _happy_ boy was eating _vanilla_ ice cream with _chocolate_ sauce.

8. In my grandmother's _country_ house I could smell a _delicious_ pie baking.

9. On Monday morning the woman wore a _blue_ blouse and a _checked_ skirt.

10. She had _black_ shoes and a _new_ pocketbook.

EXERCISE 80

1. My house /is green.
2. The supper /was delicious.
3. The boys /were noisy.
4. Your picture /is beautiful.
5. The weather /was hot.
6. But the evenings /were cool.
7. I /am busy this week.
8. That school /is big.
9. My boss /is strict.
10. But she /is fair.

EXERCISE 81

1. My house /is white with green shutters.
2. My rattly old car /was blue.
3. His new convertible /is red with a black top.
4. The cool cotton dress /is blue and white.
5. The young people /were happy and noisy.

6. I / am sad and lonely tonight.

7. We / are crowded in our small apartment.

8. The park / is lovely in the warm spring weather.

9. The busy highway / is full of speeding cars.

10. The giant plane / is high over the gray storm clouds.

7. blue *bluer* *bluest*

8. pale *paler* *palest*

9. tiny *tinier* *tiniest*

10. tame *tamer* *tamest*

EXERCISE 82

1. I am taller than my brother. **2**

2. My father is the tallest in the family. **3+**

3. You are the nicest person I know. **3+**

4. My brother is much older than I. **2**

5. She has the cutest baby I ever saw! **3+**

6. Selma and Judy are both pretty but Judy is prettier than Selma. **2**

7. A quarter is larger than a dime. **2**

8. Tokyo is the largest city in the world. **3+**

9. My sister is the best lawyer in town. **3+**

10. The World Trade Center is higher than the Empire State Building. **2**

EXERCISE 83

1. great *greater* *greatest*

2. gentle *gentler* *gentlest*

3. high *higher* *highest*

4. lovely *lovelier* *loveliest*

5. smart *smarter* *smartest*

6. funny *funnier* *funniest*

EXERCISE 84

1. *a* tree

2. *an* apple

3. *a* table

4. *an* ocean

5. *an* elevator

6. *a* pencil

7. *an* automobile

8. *an* honor

9. *a* lamp

10. *an* Indian

EXERCISE 85

1. The apples from his farm are best.

2. She wore a little red bow in her blond hair.

3. I hope you are better today.

4. You are a bad dancer but your sister is worse.

5. The ice cream vendor pushed his little cart.

6. We had delicious beef, fried potatoes, and green beans.

7. It is a good thing you have an old uncle with that much energy.

8. The TV in the next apartment makes a terrible noise.

9. I want an honest answer to my last question.

10. An eagle is faster than most birds.

EXERCISE 86

A 1. An adjective describes a _noun_ or a _pronoun_ .

2. A predicate adjective modifies or describes the _subject_ of the sentence.

3. *A* is an indefinite adjective used before words beginning with a _consonant_ .

4. *An* is an indefinite adjective used before words beginning with a _vowel or silent h_ .

B 1. The big black dog/followed the tall man.

2. A white fluffy kitten/sat on the front stoop.

3. My old grandmother/is deaf.

4. But she/is a marvelous cook.

5. In the pouring rain he/ran home.

6. He/had forgotten an umbrella.

7. My younger son/is now taller than I am!

8. Few people/are smarter than you are.

9. That boy/is the fastest runner on the track team.

10. My wife/knows which desserts I like.

C
ADJECTIVE	MORE	MOST
1. funny	funnier	funniest
2. good	better	best
3. red	redder	reddest

	MORE	MOST
4. cute	cuter	cutest
5. bad	worse	worst
6. silly	sillier	silliest
7. much	more	most
8. fast	faster	fastest
9. lovely	lovelier	loveliest
10. wise	wiser	wisest

EXERCISE 87

ADJECTIVE	ADVERB
1. loud	loudly
2. bright	brightly
3. high	highly
4. easy	easily
5. final	finally
6. silent	silently
7. usual	usually
8. close	closely
9. happy	happily
10. real	really

EXERCISE 88

1. The carpenter/hammered (noisily.) noisy

2. The child/sang (happily.) happy

3. The old lady/spoke (quietly.) quiet

4. The priest/listened (silently.) silent

5. The woman/wept (sadly.) *sad*

6. The mother/smiled (tenderly.) *tender*

7. The baby/played (busily.) *busy*

8. The dog/barked (loudly.) *loud*

9. My teacher/talks (clearly.) *clear*

10. The child/rubbed his eyes (sleepily.) *sleepy*

EXERCISE 89

1. A man/whistled (cheerfully.) *cheerful*

2. The sun/shone (brightly.) *bright*

3. A girl/sang (softly) to herself. *soft*

4. The black cat/purred (contentedly.) *contented*

5. The radio/blared (loudly) on the porch. *loud*

6. The train/roared (noisily) away. *noisy*

7. A man/skated (rapidly) across the pond. *rapid*

8. The driver/shouted (angrily) at his son. *angry*

9. The powerful car/roared (swiftly) down the highway. *swift*

10. The boat/drifted (lazily) on the calm sea. *lazy*

EXERCISE 90

1. The thief/ran (fast.) *How*

2. My son (always)/gets speeding tickets. *When*

3. I (often)/run out of money. *When*

4. The police/went (away) at last. *Where*

5. The truck driver/ate (greedily.) *How*

6. Tony/does (well) at his job. *How*

7. My boyfriend/left (early.) *When*

8. He/answered (quickly) when I called. *How*

9. I/see (better) with glasses. *How*

10. He/traveled (far) from home. *Where*

EXERCISE 91

1. The poor widow wept silent *ly*.

2. The noisy boys yell loud *ly*.

3. The men were working quiet *ly*.

4. Slow *ly* the moon rose in the east.

5. The stars shine bright *ly* in the sky.

6. He leaped light *ly* over the rocks.

7. The man spoke sad *ly* to his priest.

8. The doctor worked quick *ly* to dress the cut.

9. He has been exercising regular *ly*.

10. The mother spoke loving *ly* to the child.

EXERCISE 92

1. My friend spoke (softly) to me.

2. The workers laughed (merrily) at the joke.

3. You have (not) finished your work.

4. The boy crept (cautiously) up the stairs.

5. They moved (creakily) under his weight.

6. I wish you would listen (carefully) to me.

7. I felt (better) after I took the medicine.

8. He did (not) like to go (far) from home.

9. We (always) eat dinner at six o'clock.

10. I (often) leave the office (late.)

EXERCISE 93

1. The thief crept (silently) down the hall.

2. The phone on the table rang (loudly.)

3. He jumped (nervously) at the sound.

4. She comes (frequently) to my house.

5. I do (not always) see you in church.

6. Please do (not) yell (loudly) in the house.

7. They (often) take trips to the beach.

8. Al (never) told me about that.

9. He does (not) talk about other people.

10. But he (always) listens to them.

EXERCISE 94

1. The boy studied so hard for his exam.

2. She worked very carefully at her knitting.

3. Please come in more quietly.

4. She sang so sweetly that the baby stopped crying.

5. He shouted very loudly for help.

6. She criticizes more quickly than I.

7. Jack works much harder than you do.

8. I feel very well, thank you.

9. The lady spoke most kindly to him.

10. Please do not go so far from home.

EXERCISE 95

1. John drove _more_ carefully after his accident. (more, less)

2. Mary is _more_ dependable than Jean, who is disorganized. (more, less)

3. She works _most_ efficiently. (most, least)

4. Please come in _less_ noisily. (more, less)

5. Jim spoke _less_ rudely after I had explained things to him. (less, more)

6. She answered me _most_ graciously. (most, least)

7. The doctor operated _more_ efficiently with good lighting. (more, less)

8. His old car travels _less_ rapidly than mine. (more, less)

9. She solved the problem _most_ intelligently. (most, least)

10. She works _less_ effectively when she is tired. (less, more)

EXERCISE 96

1. Beth always behaves herself; she is a _good_ girl.

2. Beth always behaves herself _well_ .

3. John learned his lesson _well_ .

4. He got a _good_ mark on the test.

5. A _good_ man is sometimes called a saint.

6. Nancy did her job _well_ .

7. That is a _good_ book.

8. Jimmy's work in the shop is _good_ .

9. Eddie repairs cars very _well_ .

10. I feel very _well_ , thank you.

EXERCISE 97

1. Theresa did ~~good~~ in school today. *well*

2. Why don't you behave ~~good~~? *well*

3. You didn't paint ~~good~~ today. *well*

4. He did his work ~~goodly~~. *well*

5. Congratulations! You spoke ~~good~~ in the meeting. *well*

6. You learned your lesson ~~good~~. *well*

7. Jim did a ~~well~~ job. *good*

8. Jenny served the guests ~~goodly~~. *well*

9. Miss Johnson told a ~~well~~ story. *good*

10. Ted shoots a ~~well~~ game of pool. *good*

EXERCISE 98

1. A very big dog/barked at me.

2. Jimmy/was always hungry.

3. May/grew terribly fat.

4. My legs/are always tired!

5. She/looked more pleased than ever.

6. The boy/grew extremely tall.

7. We/are most happy about this.

8. Ted/ran very fast up the hill.

9. The stranger/came from a most distant land.

10. Patty/was so friendly today!

EXERCISE 99

weak	*weaker*	*weakest*
patient	*more patient*	*most patient*
kind	*kinder*	*kindest*
delicious	*more delicious*	*most delicious*
tight	*tighter*	*tightest*
happy	*happier*	*happiest*
fragrant	*more fragrant*	*most fragrant*
miserable	*more miserable*	*most miserable*
pleasant	*pleasanter* *more pleasant*	*pleasantest* *most pleasant*
careful	*more careful*	*most careful*

EXERCISE 100

1. Teddy runs fast. ~~How~~

2. The child cried often. *When*

3. The old man walked slowly. *How*

4. The door slammed suddenly. ~~How~~

5. Her phone rang immediately. *When*

6. I am very hungry. *To what degree*

7. My grandfather got too tired. *To what degree*

8. The little girl is just three. *To what degree*

9. Every day Tim grew more lonely. *To what degree*

10. The children are most excited! *To what degree*

EXERCISE 101

1. The manager spoke in a (quiet, quietly) voice.

2. Joe answered him (polite, politely).

3. He comes (regular, regularly) to my house.

4. The bull was big and (strong, strongly).

5. Janie plays the guitar (good, well).

6. Davie ate his lunch (quick, <u>quickly</u>).

7. His wife made him a (<u>quick</u>, quickly) lunch.

8. I am a (<u>slow</u>, slowly) thinker.

9. I think very (slow, <u>slowly</u>).

10. Julie's embroidery is (<u>beautiful</u>, beautifully).

EXERCISE 102

1. I am going ___to___ the park.

2. I want __to__ go, __too__ .

3. The __two__ of us will go.

4. We want __to__ go __to__ church.

5. It is __too__ hot __to__ work.

6. I have __two__ sisters, __too__ .

7. It's __too__ much trouble __to__ do it.

8. This is __too__ hard __to__ read.

9. She's __too__ busy __to__ talk.

10. The apple is __too__ green __to__ eat.

EXERCISE 103

1. __There__ is too much noise in __their__ room.

2. __Their__ office is over __there__ .

3. She is in __their__ club, too.

4. __There__ were twenty people on __their__ bus.

5. __Their__ house is too far away; we can't walk __there__ .

6. __There__ is something I don't understand about __their__ behavior.

7. __There__ are the men I told you about; they are over __there__ .

8. I left my book on the table over __there__ .

9. __There__ are too many people who want __their__ own way.

10. __There__ is no reason for __their__ critical attitude in this matter.

EXERCISE 104
(Suggested Sentences)

there is

There is no one home.

too much

He ate too much candy.

over there

She put the package over there

their wishes

He complied with their wishes.

there are

There are no children here.

to go there

He was not old enough to go there.

too many

They asked too many questions.

to church

The women walked to church.

went there

Some very famous people went there.

their customs

Their customs were strange to us.

too hot to work

It was much too hot to work.

their names

She forgot their names.

EXERCISE 105

A. An adjective modifies a *noun* or a *pronoun*. An adverb modifies a *verb*, an *adjective*, or another *adverb*. Adverbs answer the questions *how*, *when*, *where*, and *to what degree*.

B. After each of the following words, write *adj* or *adv* to indicate which each one is.

kind	*adj.*	handsome	*adj.*
gently	*adv.*	funny	*adj.*
rapid	*adj.*	lately	*adv.*
green	*adj.*	pretty	*adj.*
rapidly	*adv.*	often	*adv.*
beautiful	*adj.*	very	*adv.*
good	*adj.*	weak	*adj.*
well	*adv.*		

C. 1. Dulcie/walked slowly home from work.

2. She/was not very happy.

3. The boss/was terribly mean to her.

4. Her mother/called loudly from the window.

5. She/was almost late for supper.

6. She/did not feel very hungry.

7. Dulcie/was often lonely.

8. But tonight she/felt more lonely than usual.

9. Then the telephone/rang suddenly.

10. Dulcie/had a very nice surprise!

D. 1. very slowly _____ *adv.*

2. so heavy _____ *adj.*

3. worked hard _____ *verb*

4. slept restlessly _____ *verb*

5. much later _____ *adv.*

6. most wonderful _____ *adj.*

7. so delightfully _____ *adv.*

8. too heavily _____ *adv.*

9. studied well _____ *verb*

10. too hard _____ *adj.*

E.

rapidly	*how*	lovingly	*how*
daily	*when*	often	*when*
more	*to what degree*	away	*where*
lately	*when*	so	*to what degree*
nearby	*where*	sometimes	*when*

EXERCISE 106

1. My birthday was last Tuesday, September 9th.

2. I come from Greenfield, Mass.

3. I was born on June 30, 1962.

4. My grandmother lives at 4 Locust Lane, Springfield.

5. Do you mean Springfield, Massachusetts or Springfield, Illinois?

6. Valentine's Day is on Tuesday, February 14.

7. I'll be at the Hilton Hotel, Los Angeles, California.

8. You can reach me there until Wednesday, March 18.

9. I'll be back home on Friday night, March 20.

10. My address is 16 Ridge Road, Arlington, Virginia.

EXERCISE 107

1. Well, shall we get started?

2. Yes, it's about time we did.

3. I'm afraid, however, that we will be late.

4. Oh, no, I don't agree with you!

5. Well, we shall see who is right.

6. You may, however, be surprised by what happens!

7. No, I don't think so.

8. Well, I could be wrong, I suppose.

9. Yes, you certainly could!

10. Oh, well, we'll soon find out who's right.

EXERCISE 108

1. Joe, please close the door. ___C___

2. I asked you, Joe, to close the door. ___S___

3. Honey, do you like this dress on me? ___Q___

4. Are you listening to me, Peter? ___Q___

5. Please get some ice, Julie, and bring it out here. ___C___

6. Sheila, would you write that letter for me? ___Q___

7. Watch out, Jim, he'll bite you! ___E___

8. I warned you, Phil, to keep your dog tied up. ___S___

9. Darling, where on earth have you been? ___Q___

10. I've been waiting for you, dear, for an hour! ___E___

EXERCISE 109

1. Our flag is red, white, and blue.

2. Today we have fried chicken, shrimps, and spareribs.

3. My favorite sports are skating, soccer, and basketball.

4. The big, brown, hungry bear headed for the campfire.

5. Dave, Ed, and Joe took off hastily when they saw him.

6. The lady was hot, tired, and cross.

7. She had been to department stores, specialty stores, and discount stores.

8. She had been jostled, bumped, and pushed around.

9. Now all she wanted was rest, peace, and quiet.

10. Instead she found her children quarreling, crying, and fighting each other.

EXERCISE 110

1. Millie, my sister, has a new dress.

2. Elizabeth II, the Queen of England, has four children.

3. Miss Cass, I want you to meet my mother, Mrs. Salerno.

4. This is my friend, Ed Mahoney.

5. The lawyer, Mr. Williams, called us to his office.

6. Our minister, Rev. Parker, preached a fine sermon.

7. My father, Jack Grillo, is a taxi driver.

8. The captain of the baseball team, Joe Murray, is my pal.

9. The tiger, a dangerous animal, does not make a good pet.

10. Paul Tribuno, the winner of the match, made a short speech.

EXERCISE 111

1. "Jimmy, where are you?" cried the mother.

2. "Jimmy," she cried, "where are you?"

3. "Come here," called the boss.

4. The boss called, "Come here!"

5. "Where is Kent Place?" the confused driver asked.

6. "Can you tell me," asked the driver, "where Kent Place is?"

7. "Turn left at the next corner," the policeman said. "It's the first street on your right."

8. "You can't miss it," he added. "There's a mailbox on the corner."

9. "Thanks, officer," said the driver, "for helping me out."

10. "Don't mention it," he replied. "I'm glad to help."

EXERCISE 112

1. Our grandmother's birthday is next Saturday, February 23.

2. "Grandmother, how old will you be then?" asked Tony.

3. We're having a party at her home at 129 14th Street, Cleveland, Ohio.

4. My mother, Mrs. Salerno, has made a big cake.

5. My cousins Tony, Joe, Douglas, and Mike are all invited.

6. Joe, however, will not be able to come.

7. "Joe, I hope you are coming to the party," said my mother.

8. "No, I can't," said Joe. "I have to go to the dentist."

9. "Well, come afterwards," suggested Tony.

10. "Yes, I could do that," said Joe. "Thanks a lot, Tony."

EXERCISE 113

1. "Waitress, can I have the meat loaf special?" asked Eddie.

2. "It's all gone but we have stew, corned beef, and fried fish," said the waitress.

3. "Oh, nuts," said Eddie. "I just feel like having meat loaf."

4. "Well," said the waitress, "how about a hamburger?"

5. "No, I had one for lunch," said Eddie.

6. "Look waitress, does the stew have dump-

   lings?"she asked.

7. "Yes, I think so," she answered.

8. "O.K., I'll try that," said Eddie.

9. "Here you are,"said the waitress. "I hope you

   like it."

10. "Thank you,it hits the spot,"said Eddie.

EXERCISE 114

1. I handed Henry the (letter.)

2. She gave the baby his (bottle.)

3. The secretary took her boss his (mail.)

4. The man left the waiter a (tip.)

5. Joe got his son a new (bike.)

6. He gave him the (bike) for his birthday.

7. Will you please pass me some (coffee?)

8. The live wire gave him a bad (shock.)

9. Mrs. Gibbs told Mrs. Murphy the latest (gossip.)

10. I gave Mr. Kirby your (message.)

EXERCISE 115

1. Marie and Debbie/ran (up the steps.)

2. They/put their books (on the table.)

3. He/took a box (from the shelf.)

4. Her sister/came (down the stairs)

5. She/invited them (into the living room.)

6. They/sat down (on the couch.)

7. We/looked (at a new book.)

8. Later they/went (to the movies.)

9. The toys/were left (on the floor.)

10. She/carried the dishes (to the kitchen.)

EXERCISE 116

PREPOSITION	OBJECT
on	porch
1. up	steps
2. on	table
3. from	shelf
4. down	stairs
5. into	room
6. on	couch
7. at	book
8. to	movies
9. on	floor
10. to	kitchen

EXERCISE 117
(Suggested Sentences)

1. A flock (of sheep)

   A flock (of sheep) grazed in the field.

2. A cap (with a feather)

   The clown wore a cap (with a feather.)

3. A man (in uniform)

A man (in uniform) was stationed (at each exit.

4. Materials (for writing)

The money was used to buy materials (for writing).

5. A prince (of royal blood)

He was a prince (of royal blood) and next in line for the throne.

4. She ran (into her house.) *adv.*

5. Jack rode his motorbike (down the hill.) *adv.*

6. Grandma's trunk is (in the attic.) *adv.*

7. She has a heart (of gold.) *adj.*

8. Susan went (through the door.) *adv.*

9. The team played (in the gym.) *adv.*

10. The horse gallops (across the meadow.) *adv.*

EXERCISE 118
(Suggested Sentences)

1. jumped (off the cliff)

The unhappy lovers jumped (off the cliff.)

2. shook (with laughter)

They shook (with laughter) during the comic's routine.

3. waited (at the gate)

His fans waited (at the gate.)

4. screamed (with terror)

The children screamed (with terror) during the horror movie.

5. woven (by hand)

The tapestry was very old and was woven (by hand.)

EXERCISE 119

1. The woman waited (at the door.) *adv.*

2. The lamb followed the farmer (to the barn.) *adv.*

3. Julie wore a sweater (of pure wool.) *adj.*

EXERCISE 120

1. A boy and a girl sat (on the beach) *adv.*

2. The girl's hair was the color (of corn silk.) *adj.*

3. The boy lay (on his back.) *adv.*

4. They both basked (in the sunshine.) *adv.*

5. The roof (of my house) is red. *adj.*

6. My evening dress (is of white chiffon.) *adj.*

7. My mother made it (in the evenings.) *adv.*

8. She cut it out (after work.) *adv.*

9. I stitched the seams (on the machine.) *adv.*

10. I got my wish (for a long dress.) *adj.*

EXERCISE 121

1. (The) (shaggy) (brown) dog/walked slowly down the road.

2. (The) (thin) (stooped) man with gray hair/leaned heavily on his cane.

3. (A) (huge) (fat) woman with a wide smile/waddles cheerfully up the steps.

4. (Two)(little) boys of eight years / raced ~~noisily~~ up the street.

5. (The)(great)(golden) sun / rose ma~~jestically~~ in the sky.

6. (A)(graceful) boat with white sails / skims ~~lightly~~ over the waves.

7. (The)(frightened) cat / leaped ~~frantically~~ for the door.

8. (A)(crying) baby / wailed ~~pathetically~~ in the night.

9. (Four) workers from the farm / jump ~~quickly~~ onto the truck.

10. (The)(big)(friendly) coach / speaks ~~encouragingly~~ in the locker room.

14. ~~onto the truck~~ jump   adv.

15. ~~in the locker room~~ speaks   adv.

EXERCISE 122

PHRASE	WORD IT DESCRIBES	ADJ. OR ADV.
1. down the road	walked	adv.
2. with gray hair	man	adj.
3. on his cane	leaned	adv.
4. with wide smile	woman	adj.
5. up the steps	waddles	adv.
6. of 8 years	boys	adj.
7. up the street	raced	adv.
8. in the sky	rose	adv.
9. with white sails	boat	adj.
10. over the waves	skims	adv.
11. for the door	leaped	adv.
12. in the night	wailed	adv.
13. from the farm	workers	adj.

EXERCISE 123
(Suggested Phrases)

1. Mr. Blake's _Mr. Blake's dog._
2. The man's _The man's book._
3. The girl's _The girl's shoe._
4. The girls' _The girls' books._
5. The lady's _The lady's slipper._
6. The ladies' _The ladies' handbags._
7. The men's _The men's drinks._
8. Father's _Father's pipe._
9. The child's _The child's friend._
10. The children's _The children's toys._

EXERCISE 124

1. Peter's book lay on the teacher's desk.

2. The workers' mass meeting lasted a long time.

3. "Have you seen Joan's mother?" she asked.

4. His car's brakes were not working

5. Their cars' floodlights blinded him

6. The children's voices were too loud.

7. The union's rules have to be strict.

8. This is the club members' project to raise money.

9. Mr. Blake's house is on the hill.

10. Are the women's plans completed?

I'am	I'm	Where'is	Where's
You'are	You're	I'would	I'd
He'is	He's	I'will	I'll
She'is	She's	I'have	I've
It'is	It's	You'have	You've
We'are	We're	We'will	We'll
They'are	They're	What'is	What's

Negative contractions

will not	won't	have not	haven't
does not	doesn't	should not	shouldn't
do not	don't	did not	didn't
can not	can't	would not	wouldn't

EXERCISE 125

1. you are _you're_
2. do not _don't_
3. it is _it's_
4. were not _weren't_
5. would not _wouldn't_
6. can not _can't_
7. I am _I'm_
8. they are _they're_
9. we are _we're_
10. I will _I'll_
11. should not _shouldn't_
12. will not _won't_
13. does not _doesn't_
14. he is _he's_
15. I have _I've_
16. could not _couldn't_
17. where is _where's_
18. I would _I'd_
19. we will _we'll_
20. you have _you've_

EXERCISE 126

1. He is not ready to go yet. _isn't_
2. Do not you have dinner ready yet? _Don't_
3. I am as hungry as a bear! _I'm_
4. It was not a hard test. _wasn't_
5. We are not going this week. _we're_
6. I will go with you when you do go. _I'll_
7. They would not listen to directions. _wouldn't_
8. He does not understand English very well. _doesn't_
9. I can not explain the lesson to him. _can't_
10. It is a beautiful day! _It's_

EXERCISE 127
(Suggested Sentences)

1. weren't _They weren't here._
2. shouldn't _You shouldn't be here._
3. I'll _I'll call you later._
4. wasn't _He wasn't available._
5. you're _You're next in line._
6. don't _Don't do that._
7. we're _We're moving tomorrow._
8. hasn't _Hasn't he finished yet?_

9. isn't   *Isn't it over yet?*

10. doesn't   *Doesn't he have any?*

EXERCISE 128
(Suggested Sentences)

1. can't   *I can't come over now.*

2. haven't   *Haven't you eaten yet?*

3. they're   *They're almost through.*

4. you've   *You've already seen it.*

5. wouldn't *Wouldn't you like some water?*

6. you'll   *You'll like him.*

7. I've   *I've got a fever.*

8. he's   *He's going to the dance.*

9. I'm   *I'm seventeen years old.*

10. she'll   *She'll take the box.*

EXERCISE 129

1. It's very cold.

2. It's too late now.

3. It's a beautiful day.

4. Why, it's nearly lunchtime!

5. I like it because it's funny.

6. Drink this. It's delicious!

7. Now it's time to go.

8. It's going to be such fun!

9. It's hard to spell that word.

10. It's not necessary to be rude.

EXERCISE 130

1. It's time to start the meeting.

2. The bus is behind its schedule.

3. It's going to take fifteen minutes.

4. The cat chased its tail.

5. Meat loses its flavor when it's cooked too long.

6. It's a nice house; its lawn is lovely, too.

7. The cat carried its kittens in its mouth.

8. The chair has lost one of its legs because it's so old.

9. It's going to take an hour for the train to get to its destination.

10. The dog can't find its bone because it's under the refrigerator.

EXERCISE 131

1. He crawled into the cave; he looked around.

2. The teacher glanced at the clock; it was nearly noon.

3. These boys made the first team: Joe Ferrara, Tony Rocci, Henry Koch, Ed Argento.

4. The girl looked at him; she said nothing.

5. On her grocery list were written these items: apples, milk, lettuce, cereal, steak.

6. The men shouted angrily; then the women screamed back at them.

7. The manager ordered the following supplies: pencils, pads, carbon paper, tape, stencils.

8. Don't cry, Tommy; crying won't help.

9. It was terribly hot; the streets were deserted.

10. The instruments in his band were:drums, a piano, a bass sax, an electric guitar, and an electric organ.

EXERCISE 132

1. I finished the job;however,I have not been paid.

2. I wish to order the following:four lamb chops, two packages of peas,one quart of milk,and one head of lettuce.

3. These are the books I have read this year: Robinson Crusoe , The Legend of Sleepy Hollow, David Copperfield, The Last of the Mohicans.

4. My shoes are old,scuffed,and dirty;his are brand new.

5. Why,O why,can't I ever do anything right ?

6. Hear us,O Lord,when we cry unto Thee;let our prayers be answered.

7. My name is Dr.J.S.Wilson;I live at 10 Wood-ridge Road,Chicago,Ill.

8. These are my favorite foods:bananas,peanut butter, roast beef, string beans, and cherry pie.

9. When the light turns red you stop;when it is green you may go.

10. The days of the week are abbreviated as follows:Sun.,Mon.,Tues.,Wed.,Thurs.,Fri.,Sat.

EXERCISE 133
(Suggested Answers)

A. 1. *A*fter parking his car, the man *walked home*.

2. *T*he boys went out to play football.

3. *He* raced across the tennis court.

4. *G*oing to the window, Joan *opened it*.

5. *O*pening the door quietly, the mother tiptoed into the room.

6. *T*he women gave a shower for Debbie.

7. *T*he fun began when *she came*.

8. *W*hen all the presents were opened, the women *had refreshments*.

9. *T*hen they all helped to clean up.

10. *A*fter the party Kathie and Sue *left*.

C. 1. *C*hristmas *D*ay is on *T*hursday, *D*ecember 25.

2. *O*h, *I* didn't know it comes so soon!

3. *W*ell, I still have to shop for my mother, my father, and my girl friend.

4. I hope *U*ncle *O*scar arrived safely.

5. *M*y friend *P*atty has invited me to a holiday party.

6. "*I*t's going to be such fun!" she said.

7. *M*y supervisor, *M*rs. *N*ewton, lives at 83 *D*avis *S*t., *G*reenville, *M*ass.

8. *H*er daughter, *C*arol *N*ewton, is a good friend of mine.

9. *W*e were both born on *A*ug. 22, 1962.

10. *W*e did not know each other, however, until last year.

D.

1. "Tony, have you loaded that truck?" asked the boss.

2. The winter months are December, January and February.

3. It's so hot outside I had to come in.

4. Bless me, O Lord, and answer my prayer.

5. The letter is dated Saturday, Sept. 9, 1981.

6. My favorite meal is hamburgers, baked beans, and a glass of milk.

7. Our cat, a Siamese, has blue eyes.

8. Its fur is long, soft, and fluffy.

9. "I called and called," said the boy, "but nobody answered."

10. The boy's voice however, couldn't be heard over the radio's blasting.

E.

1. girls' team
2. children's toys
3. can't talk
4. men's coats
5. ladies' dresses
6. baby's bottle
7. doesn't drive
8. sheep's wool
9. haven't got
10. you'll go

EXERCISE 134

1. My parents love me (but) they get angry at me.

2. Do your work well (or) you will be fired.

3. He missed his train, (for) his taxi was caught in heavy traffic.

4. Jim wanted a new bike (but) he couldn't afford one.

5. The next Friday was his birthday (so) his father bought one for him.

6. We went to the clambake (and) Charlie ate at least ninety clams.

7. I like the meat (but) I don't want the vegetables.

8. You must practice hard (or) you won't do well.

9. We waited a long time, (for) Hal was late.

10. Then the door opened (and) he walked in.

EXERCISE 135

1. I am late. I lost my way.   *because*
   I am late because I lost my way.

2. You go now. I'll come later.   *and*
   You go now and I'll come later.

3. The game was over. I went home.   *so*
   The game was over so I went home.

4. The bell rang. No one answered it.   *but*
   The bell rang but no one answered it.

5. Mary ran to the door. She knew who was there!   *for*
   Mary ran to the door for she knew who was there!

6. Mrs. Smith took the inventory. Then she ordered more supplies.　*and*

Mrs. Smith took the inventory and then she ordered more supplies

7. Debbie baked a pie. They would have dessert.　*so*

Debbie baked a pie so they would have dessert.

8. Get out of here. Don't come back.　*and*

Get out of here and don't come back.

9. It didn't hurt at first. Later it hurt a lot.　*but*

It didn't hurt at first but later it hurt a lot.

10. I couldn't do my homework. I didn't have time.　*because*

I couldn't do my homework because I didn't have time.

EXERCISE 136

1. "Bah and humbug!" said Scrooge.

2. Lo, a miracle happened!

3. Oh, my! I almost forgot!

4. Nuts! I should have known better.

5. Whew! That was a narrow escape!

6. Alas, we must say farewell.

7. Hurray! We won the lottery!

8. Hey, wait for me!

9. Have mercy upon us, O Lord!

10. Ouch! I cut my finger!

EXERCISE 137

1. My goodness, I forgot my dental appointment!

2. Hey, where do you think you're going?

3. Good Lord, what's going on here?

4. Hear my prayer, O Lord, and be merciful.

5. Pow! Robert hit the crook hard.

6. Ding, dong, the bells are ringing.

7. Gee whiz, that's not fair!

8. The boy fired his toy gun, bang, and the bird

flew away.

9. Boy, you made a strike!

10. We won! Hurray for our team!

EXERCISE 138

What part of speech is followed by a noun, forming a phrase?　_Preposition_

What part of speech expresses excitement or emotion?　_Interjection_

What part of speech joins words and groups of words in a sentence?　_Conjunction_

1. The police in the patrol car drove down the road.

2. Ouch! I caught my finger in the door!

3. Pete and Dave fished in the river.

4. The girls on the stage sang and danced before the audience.

5. The food/was very hot, but it/was tasty.

6. The foreman/was very strict in the factory.

7. On the street, though, he/laughed and fooled with the workers.

8. I/took my brother to the circus on his birth-day.

9. Gee, we/ate lots of popcorn, for it/was de-licious!

10. I/liked all the animals, but the elephants/were the best in the show.

1. Prepositional phrases used as adjectives.
   in the patrol car.
   on the stage. of popcorn.

2. Prepositional phrases used as adverbs.
   down the road. in the door. in the river.
   Before the audience. in the factory. on the street.
   with the boys. to the circus. on his
   birthday. in the show.

3. Interjections. *Ouch!*   *Gee*

4. Conjunctions used in compound subjects and predicates. *and*   *and*

5. Conjunctions used to join two complete sentences. *but*   *for*

EXERCISE 139

1. I/love my children. *verb*

2. Love/is a wonderful feeling. *noun*

3. The children/taste the new dessert. *verb*

4. My sister/has good taste in clothes. *noun*

5. My mattress/has a broken spring. *noun*

6. All the flowers/bloom in the spring. *noun*

7. The kids/spring on the trampoline. *verb*

8. We/went to a dance last night. *noun*

9. They/dance well together. *verb*

10. I/would enjoy his talk if he/didn't talk so much. *noun   verb*

EXERCISE 140

1. I played with him during the noon recess. *adj.*

2. My mother came home at noon. *noun*

3. The dog barks at the child. *verb*

4. His bark is worse than his bite. *noun*

5. The ring of the bell woke Jerry. *noun.*

6. Please ring for the nurse. *verb.*

7. My shirt is made of cotton. *noun.*

8. Janet wore a new cotton dress. *adjective.*

9. Roger put the money in his pants pocket. *adjective.*

10. The dog pants for water because he is hot. *verb.*

EXERCISE 141

A. 1. What a beautiful day! *E*

2. It's too nice to stay inside. __S__

3. Go on out and get some exercise. __C__

4. Don't you want to go out? __Q__

5. I'll help you with your homework later. __S__

6. What are you waiting for? __Q__

7. Help me carry these packages. __C__

8. What's the matter? Don't you feel well? __Q__

9. Quick, call a doctor! __E__

10. I knew something was wrong. __S__

B.
1. peter, david, and jeff are brothers.

2. they live at 35 spring st., houston, tex.

3. peter, the oldest, was born on Apr. 21, 1965.

4. "jimmy, will you please come here?" called his friend.

5. "i can't now, joe, shouted jimmy. i'm right in the middle of this."

6. "its all right," said his friend. "i found what i wanted."

7. the minister, rev. carey, came into the room.

8. she put the camera back in its case.

9. men's shoes and ladies' hats are on the fifth floor.

10. "o lord, what am i going to do now?" she sighed.

C.
1. We went to _their_ house for dinner. (their, there)

2. Betsy has done her work _well_. (good, well)

3. It's _too_ cold _to_ go outside. (too, to, two)

4. _There_ are some good books here but this one is the _best_. (their, there; better, best)

5. Doris grows more _lovely_ every day. (lovely, lovelier)

EXERCISE 142

1. Oh, the <u>needles</u> and <u>pins</u> / are in my workbox.

2. <u>Mr. Baldwin</u>, the president, / <u>came</u> into the office.

3. The <u>clerks</u> / <u>listened</u> very quietly to him.

4. <u>He</u> / <u>lectured</u> and <u>scolded</u> them.

5. A <u>flock</u> of geese / <u>flew</u> over the trees.

6. The dark leaden <u>sky</u> / <u>was</u> heavy with rain.

7. (you)
 <u>Joe</u>, please / <u>pass</u> the bread.

8. <u>Jerry</u> / <u>is</u> the strongest boy on the team.

9. High in the sky the <u>sun</u> / <u>shone</u>.

10. There <u>is</u> / <u>Mrs. Kaufman</u>, our neighbor.

1. A singular common noun _workbox, president, office, flock, sun, neighbor, boy, team, sky, rain, bread._

2. A plural common noun _needles, pins, clerks, geese, trees._

3. A proper noun _Mr. Baldwin, Jerry, Mrs. Kaufman, Joe._

4. A compound subject _needles and pins_

5. A compound verb _lectured and scolded_

6. A predicate noun _boy_

7. A noun of address _Joe_

8. An appositive noun _president, neighbor._

9. A collective noun _flock, team_

10. A verb of being, present tense _are, is_

11. A verb of action, past tense _came, listened, lectured, scolded, flew, shone._

12. A direct object _bread, them_

13. A predicate adjective _heavy_

14. A pronoun as subject _He_

15. A pronoun as object _them_

16. A prepositional phrase modifying a noun _of geese, on the team._

17. An adverb modifying a verb _quietly_

18. An adverb modifying another adverb _very_

19. An interjection _Oh_

20. A conjunction _and_

21. A prepositional phrase modifying a verb _in my workbox, into the office_

22. Give the present tense of *flew* _fly_

23. Give the present tense of *shone* _shine_

24. Give the "most" form of an adjective _strongest_

25. Give an irregular plural noun _geese_

EXERCISE 143

A.

1. "Pete, are you going to the baseball game?" asked Ted.

2. "Who wants to watch the Mets lose again?" said Pete.

3. "Oh, well," said Ted, "it's better than staying home watching television."

4. Tomorrow is my birthday; I was born on Tues., Aug. 31, 1955.

5. When I was small we lived in Chicago at 151 Spring St.

6. My uncle's car hasn't a spare tire.

7. Dr. Spencer came to dinner on Thanksgiving Day.

8. My boss, Mr. J. T. Morris, doesn't take any nonsense.

9. Bobby's little brothers are Jimmy, Arthur, and Dick.

10. The boys' bats and mitts lay all over the porch.

B.

1. I washed the dishes and made the beds; then I vacuumed the rug. _S_

2. What a lot of work you did! _E_

3. Did your mother thank you? _Q_

4. Stop making so much noise. _C_

5. When I was ready for school

   , I left (or went, or started)

C. 1. The Pope[S] / gave[P] his blessing to the crowd.

2. The dog[S] in the last kennel / barks[P] loudly.

3. The family[S] / spent[P] Labor Day at their grandmother's house.

4. Up the quiet street skipped[P] / Julie[CS] and Judy[CS], the twins.

5. They[CS] / laughed[CP] and chattered merrily.

6. Their mother[S] / called[P] them but they[S] / skipped[P] on.

7. We[S] / are[P] the two fastest runners on the track team.

8. The boy[S] in the corner / is[P] very tall.

9. Millie[S] / wants[P] us to go with her.

10. But we[S] / are[P] much too busy.

D. 1. A proper noun _Pope, Labor Day, Julie and Judy, Millie_

2. A common singular noun _blessing, dog, kennel, house, street_

3. A collective noun _crowd, family_

4. A noun used as a direct object _blessing; Labor Day_

5. A plural pronoun used as a subject _we, they_

6. A pronoun used as an object _them, us_

7. An adverb modifying a verb _loudly, merrily_

8. An adjective modifying a noun _last, fastest, two, quiet_

9. A predicate nominative _runners_

10. A compound sentence (give its number) _6_

11. A compound subject _Julie and Judy_

12. A compound verb _laughed and chattered_

13. A verb of being in the present tense _are, is_

14. A verb of action in the present tense _barks, wants_

15. A prepositional phrase used as an adjective _in the last kennel, team, in the corner._

16. A prepositional phrase used as an adverb _at their grandmother's house, up the quiet street, with her_

17. A predicate adjective _tall, busy_

18. A noun in apposition _twins_

19. An adverb modifying an adjective _too, very_

20. A conjunction _and, but_

E. 1. policeman _policemen_

2. family _families_

3. leaf *leaves*

4. noise *noises*

5. mouse *mice*

F. 1. gave *give*

2. spent *spend*

3. was *is*

4. sang *sing*

5. chattered *chatter*

Adjective   *More*   *Most*

G. 1. proud *prouder* *proudest*

2. good *better* *best*

3. beautiful *more beautiful* *most beautiful*

4. merry *merrier* *merriest*

5. bad *worse* *worst*

H. 1. *I* am

2. *you* are

3. *He, she, it* is

4. *I, He, She, it* was

5. *You, we, they* were